Belgrade Lakes

Southwest Harbor

Ocean Point & East Boothbay

Squirrel Island

CRAM'S
Rail Road & Township Map
OF
NEW ENGLAND.
PUBLISHED BY
Geo. F. Cram.
PROPRIETOR OF THE
WESTERN MAP DEPOT.
66. Lake St, CHICAGO ILLS.
1875.

THE HAND OF THE SMALL·TOWN BUILDER

*Vernacular Summer Architecture
in New England, 1870–1935*

W. TAD PFEFFER

DAVID R. GODINE · *Publisher* · *Boston*

First published in 2014 by
DAVID R. GODINE · *Publisher*
Post Office Box 450
Jaffrey, New Hampshire 03452
www.godine.com

P. 1: Helen S. Fasset House, Ocean Point, East Boothbay, Maine, (builder unknown, 1915).
P. 2: Guest House at Bramblewood, Caspian Lake, Greensboro, Vermont, (G. D. Fowler, 1908).
P. 3: Porch at Bonney Camp, Rangeley Lake, Maine, (builder unknown).
P. 4: (left) Interior, Bramblewood, Caspian Lake, Greensboro, Vermont, (G. D. Fowler, 1908).
(right) Interior, Bedroom, Frank Lewis Cottage, Southwest Harbor, Maine (R. M. Norwood, 1923).
p. 5: Bedroom, Brickelmeyer Cottage, Randolph, New Hampshire (J. H. Boothman, 1914).
Frontispiece: W. F. Osgood Cottage, Silver Lake, New Hampshire.
P. 11: Coldbrook Fall, Randolph, New Hampshire.

LIBRARY OF CONGRESS CATALOGING IN PUBLICATION DATA

Pfeffer, W. T.
The hand of the small-town builder / by W.T. Pfeffer. -- 1st ed.
    p.   cm.
ISBN-13: 978-1-56792-329-2
ISBN-10: 1-56792-329-1
1. Vacation homes—New England. 2. Vernacular architecture—New England.
I. Title.
NA7575.P44 2014
720'.4700974—dc23
2011039927

FIRST EDITION
Printed in China

CONTENTS

To Susan Boothman Hawkins, and to my parents.

Swing, Southwest Harbor, Maine.

FOREWORD

T

AD PFEFFER'S *The Hand of the Small-Town Builder* is about memory. Nominally a study of vacation houses in a few special places in Maine, New Hampshire, and Vermont, it is ultimately about our recollections of who we as New Englanders are.

The University of Colorado glaciologist's words inform us, but his photographs go directly to our non-verbal core. Haunting pictures of rambling porches, iron bedsteads, or lupine in a meadow enchanted me before I read the text. The pictures released recollections of multi-generational screen-door summers. I imagined my grandparents along the shores of Squam Lake, where they took the family before World War Two. Here, too, is the scent of pine trees on Lake Tacoma in Maine where I went to camp as a kid, along with the briny tang of the rockbound coast. And then, I was re-living a summer with my own children in a shingled house at the foot of Mount Monadnock.

It is doubtful that this precise nature photographer meant to be our Proust. But Pfeffer powerfully evokes a sensory world. Just because we see no people in his exquisite images does not mean that they are absent. These warm depictions of unfinished pine walls, rocking chairs, and shelves with summer reading are like the empty places depicted by Edward Hopper or Walker Evans: we know the inhabitants are close by. We feel the presence of campers, vacationers, and rusticators in these houses. Look at the empty hammock at a cottage in Randolph, New Hampshire. Is there anyone who has spent a summer in New England who cannot imagine what has gone on before and what will happen a few moments later on that porch?

As a three-year-old summering in the White Mountain village of Randolph, Tad Pfeffer noticed light and patterns. Despite training in the earth sciences, his brand of architectural history goes beyond recitation of the names of famous architects or scholarly analyses. "These houses made me happy. They were comfortable, interesting, accessible to a child, and seemed connected to the place in which they were situated." We find ourselves in the world of long evenings, the occasional fire on nippy nights, and dips in the lake.

The Hand of the Small-Town Builder introduces us to summer house builders, Yankee jacks-of-all-trades, men like John Boothman, Robie Norwood, and George Fowler.

They were "green" long before it became fashionable, and they were "architects" who accomplished much with limited means. Pfeffer's original intention was to simply study late nineteenth- and early twentieth-century rustic houses as a prelude to building his own retreat. But he discovered much more. Beyond the grander cottages of the more famous watering places, there were generations of builders who eschewed "opulence and needless extravagance."

In unearthing housewrights who had absorbed a homegrown tradition — what

Blue Pitcher, Caspian Lake, Vermont.

another student of coastal Maine, Lucy Lippard, calls "the lure of the local" — rather than a cultivated architectural style, Pfeffer relates the broader story of Northern New England itself. This is a region resonant with Native American names: Winnipesaukee, Pemigewasset, Mooselookmeguntic, Chocorua, Ossippee. (And how wonderful to be acquainted with the first Maine Guide, Cornelia "Fly Rod" Crosby.)

Yet living north of Boston has always been about struggling to survive. The rocky soil meant a hardscrabble existence of disappointing harvests, and if your children survived the winters, they left as soon as they could for the mills of southern New England or for rich Midwestern farmland.

What kept northern New England from vanishing altogether, or at least gave it a seasonal lease on life, was tourism. Places like Rangeley Lake and the White Mountains attracted campers, fisherman, religious vacationers, and eventually a middle class that could afford extended vacations away from home. With them came the painters, writers, and academics who were inspired by the scenery and who wished to commune with nature. The camps and houses these folks built, and expounded upon by Pfeffer, comprise that legacy.

Whether inspired by the Shingle Style and the Colonial Revival, or by the Craftsman plans published in *Ladies' Home Journal* and *House Beautiful,* what these carpenters created speaks to the best of American domestic architecture. Their work reminds us that there are more meaningful goals than waging style wars with the Joneses. Useful and memorable houses are environmentally sensitive; they employ materials wisely, and they seek harmony with the landscape, rather than overpowering it. Contentment is a major benefit of working with one's hands, not to mention relying on natural materials, such as wood and stone. Pfeffer rightly refers to the influence of the pattern books of Andrew Jackson Downing, the guru of nineteenth-century domesticity. But it might do as well to recall our architect-president. For Thomas Jefferson, these houses would be worthy of his ideal citizen farmer.

Because these builders were hitherto obscure does not make them lesser contributors to the story of American architecture. These houses have an "awareness of purpose, tempered by economy." Or to mention the over-spoken and under-heeded homily, "Use it up. Wear it out. Make it do. Or do without," Tad Pfeffer is politely offering us lessons to be learned from these modest summer homes.

The Hand of the Small-Town Builder is a manifesto and an appeal. The beauty of these vacation homes is their compactness and aesthetic wholeness. The McMansions that rudely crop up on our coasts and lakeshores are anathema to Pfeffer. If you bring your televisions, air conditioners, and enough toys to fill a three-car garage, then you are not on vacation. You are bringing with you what you should have left behind. Nor will you find yourself. That sage possum, Pogo, said it best: "We have met the enemy and he is us."

In writing about houses he simply liked, Tad Pfeffer has been transformed into a wise person – a New England version of Wendell Berry. His closing words admonish us to "simplify and distill our lives, to identify and preserve essential elements and discard others. Like the houses, which became simpler without losing their aesthetic value, we can diminish our burdens without impoverishing our souls."

WILLIAM MORGAN

Albertus Dudley House, Randolph, New Hampshire (J. H. Boothman, 1903).

INTRODUCTION

THE SUMMERS of my early childhood stand out in my memory, each one distinct and separate from the others, marked not by events but by houses. We spent our summers in Randolph, a small town set in the mountains of northern New Hampshire, and over time lived each year in a different house of a group clustered around an old New England summer hotel. The town's three hotels, gone today, were the heart of its summer community a century ago, in an age when vacationers returned to the same place year after year, many of them eventually building houses of their own that they might rent to others for a part of each summer. It was in these houses that we lived, each house marking a new setting for my summer's play and exploration, and each house as solid in my memory as the wood of its walls and timbers of its roof.

I recall waking very early once and seeing faint dawn light on the pine boards and framing of my bedroom. How long ago was it? I was three years old – the house was the old Ogilby house that burned some fifty years ago, and we lived in it one summer only. In another memory, from the Folsom house, which would make me six years old, my mother read to me as I looked out from a line of three windows, facing west. Black-eyed Susans stood outside silhouetted by the dark gold light of a late August sunset, the light coming into the room, playing in blotchy patterns on the wall, distorted by the old glass. Perhaps because of the novelty of the yearly change, or perhaps only because of any child's tendency to explore, I was fascinated by each new house, by its shape and size, by the color and smell of the wood, by the twists and turns of a staircase, by odd cupboards or strangely shaped rooms, by what could be seen from each window. Most of all, though, these houses made me happy. They were comfortable, interesting, accessible to a child, and seemed connected to the place in which they were situated, connected to the forest and mountains, connected in a way that is for me even today both subtle and powerful.

As I look at these same houses now – those that are still standing and are unaltered by modernization – I still recognize the qualities I saw as a child, and others as well. Why do these houses convey such a strong sense of connection to their surroundings? Why do they give such a sense of comfort? Exactly how do these houses, a part of the environment we create for ourselves, influence the quality of our lives?

We know that we shape the environment we live in by the houses we choose to build and the way we choose to live in them; they are an expression of our values and provide concrete evidence of our presence and purpose. The houses we live in, where and how we choose to build them, reveal our interests. They reveal what we regard as beautiful and important and also what we ignore or do not value. At the same time, we are shaped by these choices; just as surely as we alter our environment, our environment alters us. Our collective construction of houses, towns, roads, and cities all influence the character and quality of our lives the same as climate and culture, although in ways that are often invisible. The subtle but potent influence of the built environment on the lives of people is the motivation for architecture; it is the difference between raw shelter and the much more complex and fulfilling constructed world that we aspire to live in. Architects – and perceptive and imaginative carpenters – strive to serve both this goal and the demands of utility. The paired ideals of aesthetics and utility, the intangible and the tangible, are not always honored or even recognized, however. It seems that in many cases (especially today) we miss the importance of the environment we choose to build for ourselves because we believe, mistakenly, that it is only we who create it, and not that our environment, once built, in turn creates a part of us.

My simple childhood awareness of an intimate link between buildings and life, between where we live and how we live, was the inspiration of the more systematic and informed study that forms the basis of this book. My original intention, starting a decade or more ago, was to record features of rustic houses that I found attractive, with an idea of someday building a house of my own with similar qualities. I was already involved in architectural photography when I started, in 2000, to photograph some of the Randolph houses for this purpose. On studying those early photographs, however, I was immediately faced with questions demanding more than a photographic record. If my objective was to capture the aesthetic quality of this architecture, exactly which features should I photograph? Were the features I identified as attractive and valuable also features that were important to the builder? How many details of the houses I photographed were fortuitous, a consequence only of luck or possibly instinct, and how many were the product of design, of intention? Who were the builders of these houses and how did they learn to build them as they did?

In subsequent years I have found the answers to some of these questions in the extensive literature of American domestic architecture, and answers to others in the history of the American domestic building industry of the late nineteenth and early twentieth centuries. To a large degree, however, answers to my questions had to be teased out of the houses themselves, from the limited plans and written records left behind by their builders, and from conversations with the very few people still alive who knew and worked with these men and could provide direct answers to questions concerning the builder's background, working style, and sense of design.

The houses I have chosen are interesting to me because they exemplify design in which the aesthetic goals are as important as, sometimes even dominating, utilitarian goals. They are, however, houses in which economic limits apply and where opulence and needless extravagance do not have a part. These are truly small summer houses, not "cottages" in the ironic and grandiose sense of nineteenth-century Bar Harbor, Maine, or Newport, Rhode Island, although those great and imaginative buildings had a strong influence on the modest houses I will describe. These are examples of the simple houses emerging in the 1870s and 1880s from formal architectural influences like the Queen Anne, Colonial Revival, and Shingle styles, but to an equal degree from informal derivatives of those styles, considered with local, truly vernacular influences. They were built to provide a summer retreat for middle-class vacationers, individuals, and families who wished to create an aesthetically rich environment and who had the means to build and own a second home, but not on a grand scale. As summer communities grew up in New England, typically on the sea coast, around lakes, or in mountains, these vacationers brought with them certain interests – fishing, hunting, hiking, sailing, artistic or intellectual pursuits, or perhaps simple relaxation and solitude – as well as aesthetic ideals and specific desires regarding their summer dwelling drawn from their own experience and their awareness of architectural trends.

After working in Randolph for a time, the scope of my project broadened geographically into a study of houses built between ca. 1870 and 1935, and ranging across Maine, New Hampshire, and Vermont. I chose this interval because it overlaps, and follows, the period of great creative developments in American domestic architecture in the last decades of the nineteenth century. I chose northern New England because it is near the places where those architectural developments occurred, and where the growth of tourism and summer colonies occurred somewhat later than in southern New England. I chose summer houses because their

D. Young Cottage, Randolph, New Hampshire (J. H. Boothman, 1924).

designs appear to have evolved easily and quickly, possibly due to the more casual character of summer life and possibly because they were typically of simpler and cheaper construction than their year-round counterparts.

Even within this limited geographic region, however, my choice of houses has been selective. I have confined my attention for the most part to houses that fall in a narrow range between primitive shelter and "styled" houses built exactly from an architect's plans, possibly under the architect's supervision. What occurs within this range is what interests me most: the conscious reexpression of the rich mother lode of late nineteenth-century American architectural vernacular styles, constructed by local builders from distinct traditions whose design sense was formed by experience and observation and for whom both ideas and building methods were advanced by the rapid growth of technology and communication.

D. Young Cottage, Randolph, New Hampshire (J. H. Booth-man, 1924).

The evidence of the summer houses from this era that stand today show that their builders – the other subject of this work – responded generously to their clients, contributing a great deal of their own ingenuity and aesthetic imagination to create a variety of styles ideally suited to their client's needs and purposes. I have deliberately focused my attention on houses where simplicity is more evident than cultivated style, and especially on those where the direct hand of the architect is absent, where instead the rich architectural world of nineteenth-century New England was absorbed into local consciousness, idiom and tradition, to reemerge, sometimes decades later, at the hands of local builders and craftsmen who built a new vernacular style of houses with great imagination and sensitivity, but simply, economically, and without pretense. In the search for these houses I have also deliberately sought their builders. The memory of the builders has in most cases proven to be far less durable than the houses they built, but I have been able to discover a few locations where not only is the identity of the builder known but aspects of his building practices are preserved in records and drawings. In certain cases I have discovered correspondence or interviewed people who knew the builder. From these sources I have attempted to come to an understanding of how and why the houses look and function as they do. This is the true purpose of this work: exactly how do these houses convey their sense of connection and comfort, and what thoughts, experiences, and training led their builders to achieve these goals in such simple terms?

Beyond simply admiring or imitating these houses, we may draw lessons from them: how do we create houses (not just summer houses) that support and improve our lives, that truly meet our aesthetic desires and serve our needs, and still do these things efficiently and within our means? The designers of many modern houses (and buyers as well) may confuse bigger with better, and fail to recognize the subtleties of design that make a house truly livable. The evidence of this is plain in the tens of thousands of houses built annually in the United States today, growing each year in size, and composed of aesthetically cold spaces too large for domestic life, put together in arrangements that reflect efficient and cheap construction more than the needs of the people who will live there. We can do better than this. The modest summer houses of a century ago offer ideas and inspiration that have not been fully recognized or put to use; we can learn from these houses and bring forward from a century ago the creativity and sensitivity that fostered a generation of dwellings whose strengths lie in good design and awareness of purpose, tempered by economy.

Finally, the houses I have photographed and studied are by no means an encyclopedic catalog. Houses of similar age and lineage can be found elsewhere in northern New England and in other parts of the United States and Canada as well. However, life is short. I have houses sufficient to tell my story, and the reader will forgive me if I stick with the region I know best.

NEW ENGLANDERS
IN SUMMER

E VERY AMERICAN summer community follows certain traditions that vary from
one place to another, but all ultimately share a common background, derived
from general historical and architectural precedents that developed in the
United States over the past 170 years. It is easier and more satisfying to understand
the significance of these houses and communities within this context rather than
admiring them in isolation. Early on in this work, when I looked at a house in
detail, I might see an attractive window that worked effectively in the architectural
scheme of the house. Subsequently, however, I learned to think not only of that
particular window but of the mill many hundreds of miles away that produced it, of
the railroad system that brought it to its final destination, and of the entire evolution of economy, society, and technology in mid-nineteenth-century through early
twentieth-century America that enriched and enlarged the resources available to
builders, brought vacationers to their remote destinations, and even made the summer vacation possible. Here, and in the following chapter, I explore what to me are,
at least for my purposes, the most relevant parts of this rich and complex history.

Viewed in a broad context, the communities that created and inhabited these houses
reflect the evolution of the American summer vacation. Mid-nineteenth-century
industrialization and social change brought about changes in lifestyle, income, and
employment at the same time that railroads brought about a revolution in transportation. The possibility of a vacation from work, taken at a place distant from one's
home, was a direct consequence of these changes. In the buildings themselves the
transition from isolated vernacular traditions of the nineteenth century to a twentieth-
century national vernacular building style is visible, again brought about by transportation, the standardization of millwork and lumber, the centralization of its
manufacture, and, most importantly, the easy exchange of ideas among geographically scattered builders. The values and imagination of the builders themselves can
be seen in their simplification and adaptation of architectural designs of the mid-
to-late nineteenth century to summer use. And we can see deviations in design and
construction not only from high-style precedents but also from the New England
builder's "true" vernacular: the winter houses traditionally built in their region.

Smuggler's Notch, Green Moun-
tains, Vermont.

23

In the years during and after World War II, as the automobile and the paved highway revolutionized transportation, and as expectations of comfort and entertainment shifted toward modern sensibilities, the whole nineteenth-century vacation tradition came to an end. The old "Grand Hotels" vanished, along with the deliberate simplicity of summer cottage life, and eventually the houses themselves. Summer communities of privately owned houses exist in many locations today, but except in a handful of instances, they exist on new terms. Summer life today is no longer so deliberately a return to simplicity, the complications and tensions of "normal" workday life pushed temporarily aside. Today's summer houses for the most part have televisions, Internet access, appliances, air conditioning, and easy commutes back to civilization. Even the houses look a lot like the houses "back home." In short, summer life is a lot like winter life, only hotter. It wasn't always that way.

The growth of middle-class American summer communities in rural locations – at the seashore, lakeshore, or mountains – depended on two essential conditions, neither of which existed to any significant degree until the years of economic growth following the Civil War. First, these were the acceptance and even encouragement of periods of paid vacation for middle-class employees by their employers, and second, relatively fast, efficient travel to vacation areas from urban centers. Individuals and small groups had been exploring rural northern New England for recreation and refreshment since the earliest years of the nineteenth century,[1] sometimes for reasons of health and recuperation, but often simply to explore an uninhabited and isolated landscape. "Rusticators" and artists were making what were essentially tourist trips along the Maine coast and into the White Mountains of New Hampshire well before mid-century. In New Hampshire the Crawford family was guiding the occasional party up Mt. Washington as early as 1819[2]; the paintings of Charles Codman, established as a landscape painter in Maine in the 1820s, drew attention to both the White Mountains and the Maine coast, and Hudson River School painter Thomas Cole made his first trip to Mt. Desert Island on the Maine coast in 1844, soon to be followed by colleagues and students. John James Audubon painted in Maine in 1832 and 1833, while preparing his work *Birds of America*. In Vermont, mineral springs became popular destinations for people suffering from any number of ailments as early as 1800, with spas and entire towns to serve them appearing along the shores of Lake Champlain and the Connecticut River. Somewhat later, Vermont was "discovered" and popularized by painters and writers, and inns in the Green Mountains advertised their proximity to well-known peaks like Mt. Mansfield. By 1850 the writer and minister Thomas Starr King was spending summers in Gorham, New Hampshire, exploring the nearby northern Presidential, Carter, and Cabot Ranges. The publication in 1859 of his book *The White Hills: Their Legends, Landscape, and Poetry* pushed mountain scenery in general, and New Hampshire's White Mountains in particular, far forward in the imaginations of a much larger class of tourists who would soon arrive, carried on a wave of increased prosperity and mobility in the prosperous years following the Civil War.

The growth of tourism in different parts of northern New England varied depending upon the ease of access. Like Vermont along its bounding waterways, nineteenth-century coastal Maine was far more accessible by boat than by road or railroad.[3] As early as 1816, steamships provided commercial links between New York, Boston, Portland, also reaching points further downeast as well as some inland towns along the major rivers, well before artists and writers popularized the coastal region to outsiders. By the 1870s locations like Boothbay could be reached in an overnight voyage from New York City, allowing a busy New York business-man to join his family at their Maine vacation home for the weekend.

Away from the navigable rivers, travel to the interior regions of all three north-ern New England states was far more difficult. In the 1840s, Crawford Notch, below Mt. Washington's southwest flank, was a four-day journey by stagecoach from Boston – while people traveling the well-trodden route from Boston to Portland, Maine, had a choice of two trains per day.[4] Roads throughout interior northern New England were of poor quality at best, rocky, dusty, rutted, and reduced to mires in spring and during rainy periods in summer and fall. Railroads, however, already extended into the interior of northern New England for commerce and especially for logging, and forward-looking entrepreneurs saw the potential for increased commerce through tourism once railroad lines penetrated further and facilities were built to accommodate travelers. In 1845, businessmen in Gorham,

New Hampshire, urged the Atlantic and St. Lawrence Railroad to extend their line from western Maine along the Androscoggin and into Gorham. In 1851, the railroad arrived, to be greeted by a newly built infrastructure of a railroad station, hotels, trails, and bridal paths awaiting the first guests. The remaining six miles to Randolph was still a rough wagon road and would remain so until 1891.[5]

Conditions improved quickly, and by the 1870s, virtually all parts of northern New England were vastly more accessible than fifty years earlier. Moosehead Lake, a hunting and fishing destination in northern Maine, distant even by modern interstate highway standards, could be reached by overnight train from Boston (with sleeping cars) in 1874.[6] The western slopes of the White Mountains could be reached, via Littleton, New Hampshire, as early as 1853, and the line was extended to Jefferson Meadows, less than ten miles from Mt. Adams, in 1879.[7] At the western edge of Vermont's Northeast Kingdom, the town of Greensboro Bend, near the future summer colony at Caspian Lake, was connected by rail to nearby St. Johnsbury by 1872.[8]

Thus, changes in transportation had by this time enabled relatively fast and inexpensive access to beautiful and remote spots in northern New England, but the means for larger numbers of people to take a summer holiday were also necessary, along with a willingness to do so. In addition to the moneyed leisure classes that were occupying selected seaside spots along the coast like Newport, Rhode Island, and Bar Harbor, Maine, there were also communities composed of clergy and academics, who by the nature of their professions had the opportunity for summer vacations. And the same growth, prosperity, and industrialization that brought the railroads also created a more prosperous middle class: office and clerical workers, schoolteachers, clerks, salespeople, and mid-level managers, occupations which fifty years before either allowed little opportunity for leisure or did not yet even exist. Not only did increased income give these workers greater freedom, but the very nature of the work made absences possible. In comparison to farm work, for example, factory, office, and commercial occupations paid well and gave workers flexibility; they could leave for a few weeks, and their work could be carried on by another employee or simply suspended.

What remained was the will to leave, an acceptance of periods of leisure by a culture rooted in the Puritan ideal of industry and a suspicion of idleness. The years shortly before and following the Civil War provided this as well. First in "camp meetings" focused on moral well-being, and later at resorts devoted to health and physical well-being, individuals and families in New England and surrounding states had started, earlier in the nineteenth century, to regard time taken away from work as having certain positive aspects. With the rise of industrialization at mid-century, however, moral and physical health provided a new possibility: profitability. Factory and office managers, persuaded in part by the growing Victorian emphasis on cleanliness and the virtues of fresh air, came to see "vacations" (a word that appears to have entered the language with this particular meaning only in 1878[9]) as investments in their employees' future productivity. Vacations were particularly desirable when taken at resorts away from the city, away from temptations of the theater and saloon, and where activities could be pursued in fresh air among appropriate and congenial company.[10] With all these parts in place, the golden age of New England vacations began, with local guides, hotel keepers, businessmen, entrepreneurs, and builders – ready to serve.

House at Squirrel Island, Maine.

Greek Revival house, Lisbon,
New Hampshire, late nineteenth
century.

ORIGINS OF THE
SUMMER HOUSE

N O BUILDER ever truly works alone. Even the most isolated vernacular traditions exist within the context of their own history, and refinements in
design are adopted based on past experience. Whether architects executing
designs on paper or carpenters building directly from their imagination, the creators of the summer houses of northern New England worked within a long tradition of American domestic architecture. The stylistic origins of the northern New
England summer house vary from one region to another, but all of them can be traced
back to changes in American building practice that started in the 1840s. Local builders would probably not have recognized that historical lineage in any particular
detail, and almost certainly they would not have consciously applied any of the
architectural theory that emerged during that time. Whether or not the builders knew
the history, it is worth considering the history as we search for the essential character of these houses, for the qualities that make them work, both practically and
aesthetically.[1]

Along with social, technological, and economic change, architecture in nineteenth-
century America also underwent a profound transformation. Design principles and
tastes dictating desirable domestic architecture changed rapidly at mid-century and
afterward, as did the variety of available building materials and the relative cost of labor
and materials. In the last decades of the nineteenth century, a builder in a rural town
would have clients, and possibly summer residents among them, with interests and
aesthetic values quite different than those of a half-century earlier, and different resources
of material and information at his disposal with which to satisfy those interests.

Mid-century changes in architecture were stimulated by the writings of the American gardener and landscape architect Andrew Jackson Downing. Prompted by his
background in horticulture, Downing explored domestic architecture from an organic
and broadly aesthetic viewpoint, at least compared to the builders and architects
whose work predominated throughout the first decades of the nineteenth century.
From post-Colonial times through the 1830s, American domestic architecture was
steeped in classicism. Essentially ornamental house types including Adam, early
Classical Revival, and Greek Revival dominated building styles in the United States.

TOP: *Georgian style house, Wiscasset, Maine, eighteenth century.*

ABOVE: *House with Greek Revival elements, Maine coast, mid-nineteenth century. A simple Cape Cod-style house could be made into a Greek Revival house, or at least refer to it visually, simply by adding wide corner trim and the broad frieze board characteristic of Greek Revival entablature.*

And styles were defined primarily by ornamentation, which was applied to basic plans and layouts adopted for the most part from Colonial traditions. Particular ornaments could be applied to a wide variety of house types, with the consequence that houses could be recycled stylistically and brought up to date simply by chang ing details. The characteristics defining the Greek Revival and other styles of the first half of the nineteenth century were thus externally imposed and did not depend fundamentally on the qualities of layout, massing, or articulation[2] that defined the shape of the house and relationship between its interior spaces. The ways in which house design aided or hindered its occupant's activities, or harmonized (or not) with the landscape, were of little concern to builders before Downing's time, for most fundamental qualities had been established by tradition.

Downing's most influential works were his 1841 *Treatise on the Theory and Practice of Landscape Gardening*, followed by *Cottage Residences*, published in 1842, and *The Architecture of Country Houses*, published in 1850.[3] Downing advocated a strongly aesthetic and moral point of view that both reacted to and took advantage of the circumstances of the industrial revolution and a growing suburban population. Essentially a romantic, he envisioned a particular aesthetic setting for people, houses, and landscape, integrating all three in form and purpose. The industrial revolution made the attainment of his vision possible, since, in principle at least, it put the ownership

Downing's Design V, Workingman's Model Cottage. (The Architecture of Country Houses, D. Appleton, New York, 1850)

Prospect Farm, Lancaster, New Hampshire (1810, builder unknown. Photographer and date of top and middle photographs unknown, probably mid-nineteenth century.)

TOP: This simple two-bay farmhouse was built on the slopes of Mount Prospect in Lancaster, New Hampshire, and has remained in the same family for most of its two-hundred-year existence. Little is known of the details of its construction, but some educated guesses can be made from details in the photograph. The wing on the right side of the photo appears to be rougher in construction than the main building (no shutters, limbed trunks for porch roof supports) and the presence of repairs to the clapboards suggests that the wing is older and predates the main building. Also, note that the worn path leads to the wing, not the main door.

MIDDLE: At some point in the latter half of the nineteenth century the house was sold out of the original family and was expanded and converted to fit the then-popular Adirondack style. The house in the earlier photograph is almost completely obliterated under Adirondack trim, but it is still there.

BOTTOM: (Photo date 2009.) Ownership of the house returned to the original family around 1930, and the elaborate decorative alterations were removed, restoring the house to something approaching its original form, albeit on a larger scale. The large front-facing gable addition at the far right end of the Adirondack renovation of the house was removed in this restoration and set back as a detached barn; it is visible here in the background. The shape of the original house can be easily recognized in the modern building.

of a piece of land and a home within everyone's grasp; at the same time Downing's vision became increasingly necessary, as industrialization often presented a landscape both aesthetically objectionable and unhealthy. He broke with existing classically oriented architectural values by introducing new principles of asymmetry, angularity, and contrast in spatial organization, derived in large part from the aesthetic concept of the picturesque, a term which in his use denoted a certain irregularity and a roughness that embodied the characteristics of nature and humanity.

Downing promoted designs which considered the occupant's activities and comfort, trying to coordinate the arrangement of interior spaces both to optimize their utility and to reflect those relationships between the occupants which to him represented the ideals of domestic life. He also considered the relationship between the house and its setting, emphasizing harmony between building style and surroundings, the importance of views, and shelter from the elements. He placed great importance on "Truth" in architecture, precepts that included the use of building materials appropriate to the structure's location and purpose, and a design that honored the purpose of the building and the presence of people.

Downing's concept of the picturesque and use of asymmetry in architecture was complex and subtle but not new; neither was his accommodation of the needs and convenience of a building's occupants new, for all vernacular architecture could be expected to respond in some fashion to needs and utility. But his writings were new, in their expression of these factors as core design principles. In the balance of elements considered in "symmetry" or "asymmetry," Downing included not only visual or structural elements but also the significance of those parts, the importance of portions of a building to a viewer who knows their purpose and the sensations of occupying them. Thus tangible parts of the structure – walls, roofs, chimneys – could be balanced by voids – porches, windows, verandas – according to the viewer's knowledge of their use and meaning.

The immediate effect of Downing's three publications was the introduction into the United States of the Gothic Revival and Italianate styles. By the Civil War these had eclipsed the Greek Revival that had dominated American architecture since its introduction in the 1820s. In contrast to its fixed and formulaic structures, the new Gothic Revival and Italianate styles opened up a variety of options in design and appearance. They also initiated experimentation by builders and comparatively rapid stylistic evolution, especially in the years between 1860 and 1875. They also differed from Greek Revival in their acceptance of wood as a legitimate building material in its own right, as opposed to using it to imitate stone or masonry. Timber design in America was strongly influenced by the timber traditions of Europe and, after the 1876 Philadelphia Exhibition, by Japanese timber buildings.[4] In keeping with Downing's concern for truth in architecture, wood textures and forms were shown for what they were; important decorative elements in their own right. Furthermore, new framing methods evolved using much lighter sawn wooden members

Italianate house, Augusta, Maine, mid-nineteenth century. Timber from the Maine woods and manufacturing along Maine's rivers generated the wealth to build great numbers of imposing and high-style private houses during the mid-nineteenth century. Successful businessmen in Augusta were among those who also built summer houses along the Maine coast.

than earlier post-and-beam construction and employing newly developed wire nails as fasteners (again, the influence of technology). The new "balloon frame" method inspired a decorative element itself, with skeletal structural elements mirrored in outer cladding and decoration; this was the first truly American architectural innovation, the Stick style. The increasing availability of industrially produced millwork and the widespread publication of pattern books, which detailed floor plans, elevations, and decorative elements, enabled builders across the United States to make styled houses without the participation of an architect. The far-reaching consequence was the rise of a new kind of national vernacular style, where fashionable designs were rapidly assimilated and reinterpreted in many locations, with variations evolving rapidly depending on local traditions, tastes, and environmental and economic demands. The Stick style grew more or less simultaneously with the popularization of the Gothic Revival and Italianate, but it reached its apogee in the 1870s when it merged with the new awareness of Japanese architecture and the English Queen Anne, and came back under the sway of the architectural profession. In their hands it became the American Queen Anne style, and, with the construction of H. H. Richardson's Watts-Sherman house in 1874, the Shingle style.

The growth of various styles and developments in wood construction extended to far more than ornament. Downing's advocacy of asymmetrical design also inspired experiments in layout and massing that expanded the variety of the basic shape and appearance of houses. Formulas were for the most part abandoned, and roof lines, window placement, arrangements of interior space, interruptions in uniform, cubical massing, and the relationships between massing and the immediate landscape all became variables in an increasingly free-form philosophy of design.

Particularly significant in this development was the expansion of a central open interior space, or living hall. The interiors of colonial houses and the eighteenth-century designs that followed were typically broken up into separate rooms, closed off by doors with comparatively small corridors connecting them. This arrangement was partly due, at least in colder climates, to the presence of multiple fireplaces and the need to isolate rooms to minimize interference between fireplace drafts. In warmer climates, and with the introduction of central heating in the nineteenth century, larger interconnected and open interior spaces were more feasible. H. H. Richardson's work in the 1860s and architects working in the English Queen Anne style developed open plans, starting with the central living hall, which combined in a single space the entry vestibule, stair hall, parlor, and fireplace. Communication with adjacent rooms was through broad openings, in many cases bounded only by short partitions or pillars to indicate a break between one room and the next. Not widely employed in Stick style designs, the open plan became widespread in the subsequent Shingle style and ubiquitous in the Craftsman and Bungalow permutations that followed in the early twentieth century.

The Shingle style was arguably the great achievement of late nineteenth-century

Watts-Sherman House, H. H. Richardson, 1874. The archetype of the Shingle style. Designed by Henry Hobson Richardson in 1875–76, Richardson's design was possibly influenced by the English houses being built around the same time by Norman Shaw. Later additions were made by the firm of McKim, Mead, and White.

William Low House, Bristol, Rhode Island (McKim, Mead, and White, 1887). The "end" of the Shingle style.[5]

American domestic architecture. In it, the full potential of the open floor plan was realized, and full advantage taken of the textural properties of wooden shingle cladding and the power of enveloping wall and roof lines. The shapes and textures of Shingle-style houses expressed a connection with the landscape, and the varied and asymmetric massing (arising from renewed study of Colonial buildings, but also from Downing's influence) communicated the form of the interior space to the outside observer. Projections – bay windows, gable dormers, and towers – thrust the occupant inside the house out into the landscape, while voids – porches, balconies, portes-cochères – drew the outside viewer in. Being both experimental and so closely integrated with the physical landscape, it is not surprising that many of the most inventive and significant Shingle-style houses were vacation homes. Starting with the Watts-Sherman house in 1874, monumental examples – most of them vanished today – were built at Newport, Rhode Island, and Bar Harbor, Maine, and coastal locations in between by Richardson and other New England and northeastern architects, including Bruce Price, the firm of Peabody and Stearns, the firm of McKim, Mead, and White, and Maine architects Fred L. Savage and John Calvin Stevens. The dynamic, tensile quality of these houses and their expression of the relationship between people and their environment was the culmination of the change from Greek Revival, and the other classically oriented styles rooted in the eighteenth century, to romanticism. The shift to designs centered around people and the human functions of a house was based on principles grounded equally in aesthetics and practicality.

Bright flame that it was, the Shingle style burned itself out in only thirteen years.

The end can be marked either by the William Low house, built in Bristol, Rhode Island, in 1887, or by the H. A. C. Taylor house, built in Newport, Rhode Island, in 1885–86. Both were the products of the firm of McKim, Mead, and White; the H. A. C. Taylor house marked the abandonment of the Shingle style's free forms for the narrower, more academic, and more historically oriented Colonial Revival, while the Low house, built two years later, was a final indulgence in the Shingle style and perhaps of all examples the most compelling, even fantastic, expression of its power. In any case, the Low house signaled an end and the H. A. C. Taylor house a beginning, a re-embrace of tradition and antiquarianism, a rejection of originality. It is surprising to think that the entire evolution, from Downing's first writings to the end of the Shingle style, took place in less than fifty years.

At least that is how the architectural profession saw it. The Shingle style passed abruptly from the professional scene of high-style design, although a strong offshoot made its way west, arriving in Chicago with Frank Lloyd Wright in 1889, and in California with the bungalow architects Greene and Greene in the 1890s. In fact, the Shingle style persisted, largely out of the view (or at least not commanding the attention) of the architectural profession, in tens of thousands of houses built in the following decades by local builders across the United States.

Between 1850 and 1930, the population of the United States grew from about twenty-three million people to 123 million. Housing had to be constructed for one hundred million people in just eighty years – new homes of some sort for more than 3,000 people per day. True, many were urban dwellers, but rural and suburban numbers also increased during these years, with urban and rural populations rising

H. A. C. Taylor House, McKim, Mead, and White, 1886. Colonial Revival, and a return to tradition and historical precedent.

in equal proportion during the period from 1850 to 1900. And, in the latter decades of the nineteenth century, increases in urban populations were partially offset by the departure to newly constructed suburbs by more affluent and mobile individuals and by families following the same inclinations for cleaner and more healthful surroundings that had legitimized "the vacation" as a socially acceptable activity. This growth was facilitated by new manufacturing methods and housing materials, a change that occurred, not coincidentally, when manufacturing and transportation were undergoing booming growth. The industrial revolution in the United States was simultaneously providing the jobs to support a growing population and the tools with which to build houses on an unprecedented scale, and according to methods and precepts that would have surprised (and possibly pleased) Downing.

The emergence of a distinctively American architecture in the years between Downing and McKim, Mead, and White cultivated expectations that houses should be attractive, comfortable, and functional. The problem now became how to create houses fast enough to keep up with demand but also diverse and imaginative enough to satisfy new homeowners whose tastes and expectations had been so carefully cultivated by the architectural profession. The American public saw and appreciated the new domestic architecture, and those with the means to build a house wanted a part of it for themselves. The solution lay in a sort of mass production, not of houses, but of plans, which could be followed by carpenters who were skilled craftsmen, in execution if not necessarily design.[6]

Plans intended for distribution and repeated use by a large number of clients were not a new idea in the 1870s and 1880s – builder's guides containing generic examples of trim and detail work had been published in the United States throughout the first half of the nineteenth century by noted American builder/architects such as Asher Benjamin and Minard Lafever. Books presenting full house plans came later, following an intermediate stage of publications, like Downing's works, which dealt with houses in toto, rather than focusing on their decorative aspects, as did the builder's guides. Andrew Jackson Downing and Alexander Jackson Davis both published books[7] that presented elevations and floor plans, printed at a very small scale and evidently intended (along with an extended commentary) to provide conceptual ideas for the client rather than detailed instructions for the builder. Implicit in these books was the assumption that capable craftsmen were readily available to turn whatever the client made of the illustrations into a finished building. As the number of builders grew (and their range of abilities broadened) in the 1860s and 1870s, however, a demand arose for more detailed plans, and books appeared that not only presented more detailed information but offered to sell (separately) full working drawings and even individualized architectural consultation.[8]

This progression in publications led, logically, to George Palliser's *Palliser's Model Homes for the People*, published in 1876. Rather than a book on architecture, this was simply a catalog, printed in quantity and cheaply produced (it sold for twenty-five cents) of house styles for which plans could be purchased at prices ranging from five to fifty dollars. While Palliser was not the first to offer plans by mail, two new ideas set this publication apart from its predecessors: first, the plans and related services, not the catalog, were to be Palliser's source of income, and second, Palliser proposed that by using his services, architectural and contractual guidance could be conducted *entirely* by correspondence. A builder would be required to perform the mechanical work, but every other aspect of construction, from environmental siting and functional planning (a design "program plan" in modern terminology) to bud-

Staircase and window, D. Young Cottage, Randolph, New Hampshire (J. H. Boothman, 1924).

geting and contracts, would be provided by Palliser. The success of this booklet and its revised edition, published in 1878, confirmed the value of Palliser's approach, stimulated imitators, and ultimately caused a fundamental shift in the way popular architectural services were marketed in quantity. The evolutions that followed, such as magazines specializing in home design (most notably the *Ladies' Home Journal*, although many such periodicals attracted a wide readership and sold many houses)

Gorham House (1858), Gorham, New Hampshire. Greek Revival adapted to a commercial building.

all followed Palliser's methods to some degree. By the time that the style-setting members of the architectural profession abandoned the Shingle style, a smoothly functioning mechanism was in place to reproduce it in many thousands of houses, not just replicated but altered – evolved – in ways that responded to clients' tastes and desires and that were the fruits of local builders' imaginations and ingenuity.

Armed with these new, abundant, and highly varied sources of information, local builders continued to work with the Shingle style (and the Stick and American Queen Anne styles as well), just as they had with Gothic Revival and Italianate, absorbing and reexpressing the knowledge they received. The same kind of evolution occurred then as before, with builders freely merging and altering types, creating house hybrids, mixing what had initially been carefully segregated stylistic elements. The evolution in year-round houses occurred slowly, partly due to social standards moving more slowly than architectural ideas, but also due to the significant constraints imposed by climate and utility. Summer houses, on the other hand, offered more flexibility: they were typically of cheaper, less durable construction, and were intended for more informal summer life. Their owners were less tradition-bound in their expectations. And with tourism increasing in the northeast, a growing number of summer vacationers were settling on favorite locations, seeking a secluded spot near a lake or facing the mountains, and contracting with the nearest competent builder for the construction of a summer cottage. The Shingle style, with its compatibility with landscape and its careful integration of interior and exterior space, was (consistent with its origins) particularly well suited to their needs.

Here is the jumping-off point for the small summer houses I will present. All are obscure by the standards of Bar Harbor and Newport; all were influenced by architectural and building literature, but most involved no architect, or used a published plan only as a general guide from which the builder felt free to depart. The simplicity of these houses gave their builders a wide canvas on which to experiment with textures and forms, particularly in the interiors. Many of these buildings were adaptations and derivatives of Shingle style designs, but others were not. Nevertheless, all, by virtue of their intended use, represented connections between life indoors and life outdoors, and related to landscape in an intimate way, the more so for their (generally) small size and simplicity. The growth of these small, vernacular forms from the body of American domestic architecture was a small tendril compared to the branch that led through Frank Lloyd Wright to the Craftsman and Bungalow styles, but it was a prolific and productive one. Like a garden left to grow wild, all the parts became mixed, and while much of the structure and order of the disciplined phase was lost, other qualities arose, not least among them grace, human scale, a connection to the landscape, and (like in Downing's houses) an honest expression of architectural Truth.

Modern house with shelf returns on eaves, Berlin, New Hampshire. Certain Greek Revival elements, such as the shelf returns on the eaves seen here, persisted long after the style itself was out of fashion (in this case for more than a century) and appear in some modern buildings as vestigial reminders of an earlier architectural era.

MAINE COAST

We are in the presence of what modern architects have always said they most wanted: a true vernacular architecture – common, buildable, traditional in the deepest sense, and of piercing symbolic power.

VINCENT SCULLY, *The Shingle Style Today*

BOOTHBAY

BOOTHBAY, like much of the Maine coast, has a history of European settlement that extends back into the early seventeenth century, a time when the mountainous regions to the west were, to Europeans, still wilderness. One of the early coastal settlements, Winnegance, appeared in the area bounded by the Sheepscot and Damariscotta Rivers in the 1630s, but survived only until 1689, when it was abandoned by Europeans in the face of the sporadic violence that was the precursor to the French and Indian War. Permanent settlement did not occur until about 1730, and the region was finally incorporated as Boothbay (including the present-day towns of Boothbay, Boothbay Harbor, and Southport) in 1764.[1] Settlement of Boothbay grew throughout the nineteenth century, fostering industries in brickmaking, logging, quarrying, ice cutting, farming, fishing, boatbuilding, and, by the mid-nineteenth century, tourism.

Today, tourism is Maine's largest industry. The transition to this from Maine's mid-nineteenth-century economy, based on extractive industries and water-powered manufacture, was neither simple nor smooth, but the first stages occurred swiftly in the years surrounding the Civil War. Westward migration and the growth of railroads had enriched the nation as a whole, but northern New England suffered more loss than gain. Farmers left Maine for richer farmlands in the Midwest; manufacturing and industrial jobs vanished as improved transportation broadened markets geographically and exposed Maine to increased competition. By the time the first tourists were discovering the unspoiled beauties of the Maine shoreline, the state's coastal population was already shrinking and farmsteads were being abandoned.

A typical Downeast coastal port.

43

Those early tourists were not seeing into the past when they looked over the Edenic landscape of the Maine coast, but into a future which the region's original inhabitants would hardly have sought if they had the choice.[2]

OCEAN POINT AND EAST BOOTHBAY

Ocean Point stands out at the tip of Linekin Neck, the peninsula separating the Damariscotta River from Linekin Bay and Boothbay Harbor. The open sweep of the ocean can be admired from its shore, the view encompassing the horizon from Pemaquid Point on the east to Southport on the west, the ocean's rim broken only by a scattering of islands. It is windswept and exposed, rocky, poor of soil, and never a choice location for homesteaders who tried to farm it. But for the mid-nineteenth-century culture of summer tourism, the location was ideal: fresh air, sun, sea breezes, and ocean bathing, all of them essential parts of the health-oriented movement that justified periods of leisure and restful, wholesome social activities. In fact, Boothbay had been identified in 1837 as a "favorite resort for invalids during the summer season, on account of the purity of the air and the facilities for bathing in clear sea water,"[3] but not until the 1870s did the combined influence of improved transporta-

Lupine, Ocean Point, Maine.

tion and increased wealth allow vacationers to come for the regular and extended visits that made private summer cottages preferable alternatives to hotels.

In 1877, Dr. Leander J. Crooker of Augusta started the first development of houses expressly built as seasonal summer homes on Ocean Point. Crooker had bought a large parcel of land along the outermost shore on Linekin Neck and offered free lots to the first ten parties to build houses within a year. Ten people responded, building cottages on the high ridge on the western edge of the Point, facing Linekin Bay. Sixteen more had followed by the end of 1878, all of them built by families from the Augusta area, made aware of the opportunity from Crooker's local promotion.

Between 1894 and 1900 another eighteen cottages were built in the Grimes Cove area on the Point's southeastern corner, with owners coming from Maine and Massachusetts. For over forty years, Crooker worked to develop the Point's amenities, including the construction of a water supply and a wharf for direct steamboat access, finally, in the early 1920s, selling his remaining interests in Ocean Point to

Lovicount S. Lyon House (builder unknown, 1897, demolished 2007). Built immediately on the water's edge, the Lovicount S. Lyon House made full use of the views provided from the gables, towers, and porches that typified the Queen Anne style. The unmodified Queen Anne style here is ideally suited to its location and purpose, and no invention or hybridization of style was needed to accommodate the particular needs of summer occupancy.

Our Woodland Cottage, Albert H. Kenniston (1882).

ABOVE: *Cabin with later Gothic Revival detailing, Ocean Point, East Boothbay, Maine (builder and date unknown). The Kenniston cottage stands on or near one of the oldest developed properties on Ocean Point. The date of the original house is unknown, but elements of its construction, including wood pegging in roof purlins, are compatible with a date well before Crooker's development in 1877. The ornamental Gothic Revival details (including steep dormers), however, were probably added during the cottage building boom.*

ABOVE RIGHT: *Bedroom and dormer.*

RIGHT: *Porch detail.*

Elmer E. Newbert. A Unitarian Minister and Augusta and Ocean Point resident, Newbert doubled as real estate developer, overseeing the last significant period of development of Ocean Point during the mid-1920s. Like many other entrepreneurial founders of summer communities, he acted as real estate agent, general contractor, and mortgage lender. He offered four-room bungalows for $1,000, to be built on lots available for $200, with financing of ten percent down and $5 per month at no interest for the first two years.[4] The offer was evidently attractive, for between 1923 and 1926 another twenty cottages went up under his supervision.

Travel from Augusta to Boothbay was comparatively easy then, not overland as one would do today, but by water. Steamboat service between Boothbay and Bath had been offered on the steamer *Spray* since 1865. Starting in 1880, the city of Augusta, thirty miles up the Kennebec River from Bath, was served by the steamer *Islander*, running in summers from Gardiner to Boothbay Harbor with stops at resorts along the way.[5] The last leg of the trip could be the hardest: early Ocean Point residents disembarked at East Boothbay, at the inland end of Linekin Neck, and then were carried the remaining four miles by wagon on a rough private road to Ocean Point. By the time the *Islander* started running, however, Crooker's wharf was in place, and, by taking one more boat from Boothbay Harbor, the trip from Augusta could be made smoothly and quickly, allowing a harried Augusta businessman to depart on a Friday afternoon and join his family that evening, already established for the summer in an Ocean Point cottage.

Levi Hallowell and William Allen Cottage, Ocean Point, East Boothbay, Maine (builder unknown, 1897). Main room. Purlins supporting second-story floor joists reduce the need for interior bearing walls and allow for larger rooms, although the framing in this case is unusually light.

Levi Hallowell and William Allen Cottage, Ocean Point, East Boothbay, Maine (builder unknown, 1897). The Hallowell-Allen Cottage was built on a very steep slope – virtually a cliff – on a very small lot. The constraints of the location would have limited the builder's freedom to conform to any established style, and the resulting structure is a hybrid composed of generally Victorian elements combined with shingle cladding and a few Shingle Style details (note the flared shingle skirt at the base of the porch). The massing is dictated by the confined and steeply sloping site. The utilitarian composition and harmonious but muted exterior here echoes cottages in other locations where outward presence and style is secondary to function.

The architecture of the early (1876–1900) Ocean Point houses reflects the awareness of both clients and builders of the prevalent architectural fashions of the day, viewed from a slightly conservative perspective. Massing, layout, and most ornamentation are rooted in the Queen Anne style, with certain details of cladding and ornamentation drawn from Gothic Revival, Shingle, and even Adirondack sources. Although the Shingle style was in full bloom by the late 1870s and early 1880s at Mt. Desert Island, a hundred miles to the east, it was in its early, experimental, and wild phase,[6] and the more traditionally established styles seem to have appealed most to conservative clients from Augusta. Shingle style examples and influences appear in the later Ocean Point houses. All are typically light in construction, and generally modest in size and finish, consistent with the pattern of small lots and comparatively small buildings established in Crooker's day. The houses also reflect the importance placed by Ocean Point summer residents on their setting, with windows and porches facing the ocean view. Many of the houses are light in color and often clapboarded, typical of the Queen Anne style; only later as the influence of the preromantic styles fell further away did darker colors and shingle cladding predominate. Unlike the Shingle style, with its preoccupation with connection to the ground and integration with its setting, Ocean Point harkens back to the days of Greek Revival

Helen S. Fasset House (A. S. Dodge?, 1915).

ABOVE: *Sleeping porch. Sleeping porches were a ubiquitous feature of summer cottages (as well as in year-round houses in warmer climates) in the days before air conditioning. The sleeping porch is exposed to the elements much more than the house's interior, and its construction is accordingly even simpler than the typically utilitarian finish used in so many cottages. There is more to the rusticity of this sleeping porch, however, than mere utility. Here is one of the connections between interior and exterior, between domesticity and nature, that is vital to the spirit and function of the small summer house. This relationship was explored more consciously in later architectural developments but is no less effective here for being (most likely) a simple economic expedient.*

LEFT: *Fireplace with beachstone facing.*

Keystone Cottage, Edmund Metcalf Clapp house (builder unknown, 1893), main room. The rich tone of the wood is probably purely the result of aging – softwood interiors were routinely left entirely untreated and darkened with age. The appearance of the interior of such houses must have been very different when they were first built.

and earlier, when farmers and fishermen across New England were at work pacifying the landscape, proudly proclaiming their new presence in bright white houses.

Despite my search for builder's identities, the designers and carpenters of the Ocean Point houses remain unknown. While Crooker and Newbert were both involved in land sales, neither was a builder himself, and it is unlikely that any specific designs beyond general expressions of style ever originated from either man. One of the best ways to identify a builder is through lumberyard markings on wood: at the yard, a worker would label a board on the top of a stack of lumber ready for delivery with the name of the consignee of the shipment (the person paying the bills, who was typically the contractor) and the destination. That board would generally find its way into the house, often in a position to be discovered later and often mistaken for the builder's own signature – giving rise to the widespread belief that certain builders, like artists, signed their works. The vast majority of names written in houses, however, are merely delivery labels, and often refer to people now unknown. They appear in a few of the Ocean Point houses but only hint at a history.

Keystone Cottage, Edmund Metcalf Clapp house, Murray Hill, Maine (builder unknown, 1893).

ABOVE: *Contrasting trim, a clapboard-to-shingle transition at the second floor, and novelty shingles give this simply massed cottage an ornate look. The curved dome roof over the porch was originally covered in sailcloth.*

RIGHT: *Bedroom and dormer framing detail. The interior has been carefully and imaginatively paneled in this room, leaving the frame partly exposed and partly concealed. Note how the boards in and near the dormer stand behind some framing elements and in front of others. The builder clearly intended to use paneling and trim to create a finished appearance in this room, but at the same time deliberately exposed timbers in the dormer and sloping roof to add a rustic or informal element.*

BELOW: *Helen S. Fasset house (A. S. Dodge? 1915). Door edge addressed for delivery to A. S. Dodge, inferred but not confirmed to be the builder. Boards marked with the builder's name frequently end up in a visible position in a house and are sometimes mistaken for the builder's own signature. In rare cases, however, builders deliberately left signatures somewhere in the house identifying it as their own work (see, for example, page 150).*

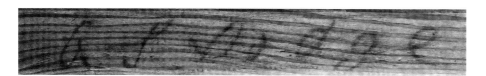

SQUIRREL ISLAND

Old Man's Beard, Squirrel Island,
Boothbay Harbor, Maine.

Sometimes on The Island, in down Maine,
in late August, when the cold fog blew in
off the ocean, the forest between Dingley Dell
and grandfather's cottage grew white and strange.

ANNE SEXTON, "Kind Sir: These Woods"

Regarded from the coast, even at the water's very edge, the Atlantic Ocean is another world from the land – the domain of fish, birds, and fishermen. There is no transition at the border between those lands; one is either firmly connected to rock and soil, in the world of field, forest, and the more or less durable works of man, or floating on the mutable and anonymous sea, everything impermanent and in motion. Except on the islands.

Squirrel Island, when covered in fog and surrounded by the sounds of wind, waves, birds, and bell buoys, can seem as untethered and mobile as the ocean itself. The island is small – a half hour walk will take you from one end to the other – and far enough from the shore to feel more a part of the ocean than the land. Yet it is rock and soil, with forest, fields, and houses, and like many of Maine's coastal islands, it has been put to use by people for centuries. The isolation of the islands provided natural fences, making them logical places for grazing animals, and they have been used for that purpose since the arrival of Portuguese fishermen early in the sixteenth century. Squirrel Island has been occupied continuously since the late nineteenth century and was farmed for nearly one hundred years before being sold in 1870 to a consortium of seven prominent Lewiston residents who had been previous summer visitors at Boothbay. This group, led by a grain and flour merchant named Jacob B.

Dingley Dell, Squirrel Island, Boothbay Harbor, Maine. (Frank L. Dingley, date and builder unknown.) Dingley Dell is an architectural fantasy composed of Queen Anne and Shingle elements. The house's dramatic exterior shapes and normally large architectural elements rendered at a very reduced scale (the corner turrets, for example, are barely four feet in diameter) are consistent with the shape and scale of the island itself, including the many dwarfed trees, battered by weather, bent and twisted from their natural shapes but clinging tenaciously to the island's rocks.

Dingley Dell, Squirrel Island, Boothbay Harbor, Maine.

ABOVE: *Dish cabinet with woven latticework. This is a built-in cabinet, evidently part of the original construction, and further evidence of the builder's (and Dingley's) imaginative design sense.*

LEFT: *Dining room. This room spans the entire depth of the house and terminates in matched arch windows at both ends; the horizontally oriented beadboard paneling increases the sense of depth. Curved surfaces and built-in benches create a ship-like atmosphere. The tie rods across the ceiling add support to the very long spans of the two ceiling joists and were probably added sometime after the initial construction of the house.*

Tetreault Gray Cottage, Squirrel Island, Boothbay Harbor, butler's pantry. Throughout the latter part of the nineteenth century, the kitchen of middle-class American homes (as well as the homes of the rich) was principally the domain of domestic servants. The distinction between employers and employees was manifested physically by architecture, and perhaps nowhere in the house were both the links and barriers between the two groups more evident than in the butler's pantry, which served in part to isolate the kitchen from the dining room. One of the principal challenges today in remodeling and renovating houses from this period is the removal or adaptation of various design features, like the butler's pantry, which segregated parts of the house used for socializing from the parts used for service, including what is today often the most "social" room of all — the kitchen.

Ham, included Bates College President O. B. Cheney and Maine representative (and future Governor) Nelson Dingley Jr. The group bought the land for the purpose of controlled development of hotels, summer houses, and facilities for a summer community. The Island was built up rapidly, with the construction in the first two years of fourteen cottages, boat landing, boardwalks, and a bowling alley. By 1906 the island had grown to 115 houses and a summer population of nearly 1,000.

Being an island, Squirrel's needs and the seasonal and daily pace of life are slightly different than the mainland. There are no public roads or automobiles; residents move around the island on foot, following a network of paths and boardwalks.

Excursions off the Island are timed to the schedule of the ferry *Novelty*, and life on and off the island is clearly delineated, not only by the surrounding water and the rhythm of the ferry schedule, but also by Squirrel's traditions and strong sense of identity.

Squirrel Island was designed as a summer-only community from the outset, and except for its caretaker and carpenters commuting from Boothbay, the island is empty in winter. The island's electrical power and water are supplied by lines originally laid in 1920. After the water supply from the mainland has been turned off in the fall, the water level in the Island's small water tower drops; when it falls past half-full, summer residents must close up their houses, roll their belongings down the boardwalks to the dock, and head home for the winter.

As at Ocean Point, the builders of the Island's houses are largely unknown, although at least a few early owners appear to have been intimately involved with

Tetreault Gray Cottage, Squirrel Island, Boothbay Harbor (builder unknown, 1905).

ABOVE LEFT: *Main room. To create a more open and unobstructed space on the ground floor, the rafter in the main room ceiling is supported from above by a steel rod system hung from the hipped roof center two floors above.*

ABOVE RIGHT: *Dining room with beadboard ceiling and walls.*

LEFT: *Bedroom. Children living here once called this bedroom "the skating rink," referring to its very large size. As in most summer houses, the interior finish on the second floor here is far simpler than on the ground floor.*

Tetreault Gray Cottage, Squirrel
Island, Boothbay Harbor.

ABOVE: *Porch view.*

RIGHT: *The house is very firmly
Shingle style in its design, but
simplified – reduced to the most
essential elements and, with the
exception of the shingled arches
supporting the porch, nearly
devoid of exterior ornament. The
house anticipates the modern
resurgence of the Shingle style,
nearly seventy years later, in Robert Venturi and John Rauch's
landmark Trubeck and Wislocki
Houses.*

Bowman Cottage, Squirrel Island, Boothbay Harbor, Maine (builder and date unknown). The Bowman Cottage was the summer home of Edmund Morris Bowman (1842–1913), a well-known organist, choir director, and music educator. The house occupies a high position in the island and looks out onto the ocean from an abundance of porches, balconies, and windows.

the construction of their cottages. Island founder Nelson Dingley Jr. advocated a rustic style and was said in a 1921 account to have judged a prospective builder who thought of using planed lumber in his cottage as "too much an exquisite for our colony."[7] Dingley's early island cottages (he and his brother Frank L. Dingley built at least four) followed these principles of simplicity. Both Dingley and Ham had spent previous summers camped in tents at Boothbay and were quite prepared to maintain equally simple quarters on their new island, Dingley's idea being "to get under a roof where they could keep dry and so he built with rough lumber, the partitions being sheets and blankets; later he made changes for more comfort."[8]

Judging from the houses on Squirrel Island today, those changes for comfort were made in short order, but not to the extravagant lengths seen in some other locations on the Maine coast. Development on the Island underwent a significant shift with the arrival of Boston furniture maker A. H. Davenport, who built more than twenty houses there between 1888 and 1903. Davenport took Squirrel Island's architectural motif out of its rough lumber and blanket phase, introducing center bead and edge bead interior paneling – a staple on many coastal Maine houses, but less common inland – and developing a more ornate style, slightly hybridized but derived directly from Queen Anne and Shingle forms. This hybridization of style

Bowman Cottage, Squirrel Island, Boothbay Harbor, Maine.

ABOVE: *Birchbark-paneled game room, installed in the 1920s by a later owner.*

RIGHT: *This central, ground-floor living room, wrapped on all sides by a second-floor balcony, forms the focal point of the house's interior and once contained Professor Bowman's organ. A sense of communal activity and shared presence is created by the circular symmetry of the main room and the direct connection between this room and most of the house's other rooms; in combination with the strong visual connection to the outside, the overall sense of the house is one of intimate contact with the elements from within the protective boundary of encircling walls.*

and imaginative departure from established forms is especially well represented by "Dingley Dell," built by Frank L. Dingley.

The framing and foundations of Squirrel Island houses are frequently lightly built, a widespread practice for summer-only structures in regions with light winter snow loads and perhaps more so on an island where the effort and expense of moving lumber was greater. Local builders repairing Squirrel Island houses today encounter framing methods that suggest fast construction and absence of detailed drawings – again routine for summer houses of the period, and consistent with Squirrel's rapid early development. But the layout and general architectural character of the houses show an understanding and appreciation of contemporary architectural styles combined with an acute awareness of the setting. Here, as elsewhere, frugal construction seldom excluded fundamental aesthetics.

Squirrel Island, Boothbay Harbor, Maine.

Southwest Harbor, Mt. Desert Island

Mt. Desert Island – so close to the mainland that it is barely an island – was named in 1604 by Samuel Champlain, who sailed into Frenchman Bay, on the island's east side. It was on Mt. Desert Island that Jesuits established the Saint-Sauveur mission in 1613. The Jesuits had placed missions along the Atlantic coast from Nova Scotia to Maine to convert native people to Catholicism and to study the native cultures; at Saint-Sauveur, the priest Pierre Biard worked to understand the language of the local Wabanaki people, so they might be instructed in the Catholic faith before being baptized. However, the area was a part of the region contested by the British and French, and the French mission came under attack almost immediately by the British Captain Samuel Argall of Virginia and was abandoned not long thereafter.

Permanent settlement did not come to Mt. Desert Island until 1760, as the end of the French and Indian War drew near. Abraham Somes built a cabin at the site of what is now Somesville, went back to Gloucester, Massachusetts, to gather his family, and returned the following year. He had chosen the head of a deep and sheltered inlet in the island for his homestead – Somes Sound, the only true fiord on the East Coast.

Somes Sound splits the island nearly in two and is one of six glacial troughs that define the landscape of Mt. Desert Island. During the nineteenth century, Somesville developed as one the island's commercial centers, along with the settlements of Southwest Harbor and Northeast Harbor that flank the Sound at its mouth. Bar Harbor grew up on the east side of the island, facing Frenchman's Bay. As elsewhere on the Maine Coast, tourism came to Mt. Desert Island in the mid-nineteenth century, led principally by artists rather than seekers of health as at Boothbay. Hudson River School painters Thomas Cole and Frederick Church presented Mt. Desert Island in glowing imagery to a public already highly receptive to romantic interpretations of natural landscapes and rural life, an aesthetic reinforced by Henry David Thoreau's writings and Downing's work in domestic architecture. The summertime arrival of increasing numbers of "rusticators" to Mt. Desert Island filled the available rooms of local farms and by 1855 led to the first hotels, and by 1868, the first cottages. The rusticators were a breed who not only sought healthy, simple, rural settings for their vacations but also an intimate relation with and understanding of the landscape. Their interests included aesthetic, scientific, and intellectual pursuits, all best served by accommodations harmonizing with their environment. Theirs were houses that reinforced the connection between man and nature, between domesticity and wilderness, between life indoors and out. Here again is the recurring theme of the small summer house: simplicity, unobtrusiveness, natural, locally derived materials and textures, and the fine integration of shelter and exposure.

As the history of Mt. Desert Island, architectural and otherwise, bears witness, the rusticators didn't have the place to themselves for long. Bar Harbor is, with Newport, Rhode Island, the location most strongly associated with the grand summer "cottages" of the very rich, a leisure class of summer tourists who followed the rusticators to the Maine coast, bringing with them a different but related aesthetic sensibility. The occupants of the grand "cottages," like their wealthy counterparts in the Adirondacks, saw little point in abandoning luxury during the summer, but were sensitive nonetheless to the landscape they occupied and could be moved by architecture displaying a similar sensitivity. Their enormous, intricate, and stylish houses were at the center of the development of the 1870s Shingle style. Certain of

Atlantic Ocean and Great Gott Island near Ship Harbor, Mt. Desert Island.

its practitioners, such as the Northeast Harbor architect Fred L. Savage, held on to the Shingle style for several decades, designing houses either squarely in that tradition, or based on its concepts.[9]

The Shingle style (as well as other contemporaneous architectural developments) was absorbed, less famously, by a number of relatively unknown but perceptive local builders along the Maine coast and elsewhere who implemented the forms and ideas into the small cottages built for summer visitors. Bar Harbor was by no means the only place on Mt. Desert Island where summer visitors made seasonal homes. Southwest Harbor, on the Island's far side, facing the protected waters of Somes Sound, had its own summer colony, drawn initially from academic communities in the Northeast. Groups of summer houses were established in the 1880s on several parcels in Southwest Harbor (referred to at that time as Tremont), including Fernald Point, the site of the 1613 Saint-Sauveur mission. The community's connection to academics may have originated with Charles H. Fernald (1838–1921), great-grandson of Andrew Tarr, the first settler to build on Fernald Point (in 1784) after the brief occupation by the French 170 years earlier. As a young man, Fernald worked on boats, serving as a master's mate during the Civil War. When not at sea, he pursued academic studies, and by the close of the Civil War he was a student of Louis Agassiz at the latter's short-lived Anderson School of Natural History on Penekese Island in Buzzard's Bay. Fernald eventually became an entomologist at the Massachusetts Agricultural College but retained his connection, and his property, at Southwest Harbor.[10] The details of a link between Charles Fernald and the later summer community are missing, but the potential for a connection is strong, given the development of that community on Fernald's land and his connection with academics, including Agassiz, who not only had visited Mt. Desert during his own scientific studies, but, like the painters Cole and Church, knew and valued it principally in terms of its landscape.

ROBIE M. NORWOOD

Robie M. Norwood (1873–1955), Southwest Harbor, Maine.

Chief among the builders of Southwest Harbor was Robie M. Norwood (1873–1955). Typical of Maine land-bound tradesmen of the period, he never traveled far from his home (he was born at Seal Cove in the town of Tremont), but was perhaps atypical in having a keen sense of design, an awareness of ongoing developments in architectural style, and a willingness not only to build but to design buildings in a wide variety of styles. Norwood had no formal education beyond the eighth grade, and he presumably learned from a local builder[11] whose identity is unknown. Early in his life he worked as a carpenter across the Sound, walking each day out to Fernald Point and rowing across to Northeast Harbor, where Fred Savage was already well established in his own building career. There is no evidence that Norwood ever worked on any Savage house, but during the period from 1890 to 1895, Savage was commissioned to design at least twenty-three houses in Northeast Harbor alone. Working as a carpenter in Northeast Harbor around 1890, Norwood would surely have been aware of them. Norwood eventually opened his own shop in Southwest Harbor and in 1906 he built his first contract house.[12] More than two dozen of his houses are documented in the Southwest Harbor area today.

Norwood ran a large and ambitious operation, supplementing a small full-time crew with many day-laborers. During his most productive years he could supervise the simultaneous construction of several houses, moving from one job to another, checking on his principal carpenters and managing the ordering and delivery of supplies. Norwood also maintained a large storage yard and shop, buying materials in large quantities and often reselling to other local builders. Millwork (door and window units, moldings, and other materials requiring careful sizing and fitting of small members) was widely available from industrial manufacturers at this time, but Norwood nevertheless found it cost-effective to manufacture his own millwork in his shop, another indication of the scale of his business.[13]

When framing a house, Norwood used a standard three-man marking/cutting/nailing crew, with the head man (often himself) measuring and marking lumber for the cutter, who, after cutting the piece, handed it to the nailer for assembly. In addition to working from detailed plans, Norwood – like most builders of his day – was capable of laying out and assembling an entire building with minimal prior planning or drawings. In the late nineteenth and early twentieth centuries, building materials were not standardized, and the present-day practice of designing in four-foot units was not widely employed (although stock dimensional two-inch lumber and sixteen-inch stud spacing was becoming common[14]). As a consequence, the precise positions of joists or studs had little influence on subsequent steps in the construction, and careful planning and measurement to ensure precise placement of all members was largely unnecessary.[15] Framing carpenters of this time were fully capable of constructing complex mitered joints without drawings or any additional tools beyond a handsaw and framing square. One of the most versatile tools in a carpenter's box, the framing square, enabled carpenters to quickly and efficiently measure and cut roof rafters, stair stringers, and complex gables and roof intersections. These skills still exist today, but the complex framing and especially roof constructions that were ubiquitous a hundred years ago are now regarded as expensive and time consuming operations reserved mostly for larger and more expensive houses. Their presence on all but the most modest houses of a century ago testifies to the standards of skill attained by the vast majority of carpenters of that time. Morris Norwood, a relative of Robie Norwood's and member of his crew in the 1940s, described being invited by him to come to Norwood's house in the evenings one winter to "learn the framing square." The lessons lasted three months.[16]

Judging from anecdotes and surviving correspondence, Norwood enjoyed the confidence of his summer-resident clients to such a degree that a person wanting a new house built would leave him for the winter with some general ideas and a rough budget, and ask him to develop a design consistent with those ideas and budget, build the house, and have it ready for their occupation the following summer. Norwood also acted in a wide variety of other capacities for the summer visitors, supervising maintenance of the cottages in the owners' absence, finding summer help, and acting informally as the owners' advocate in real estate transactions. He also bought and sold land and buildings himself, often (again, typically for his time) financing his clients' mortgages personally.

Norwood's houses are well documented[17] and give a view of the evolution of his design skills as he advanced from executing architect's plans in the first decades of the twentieth century to building his own work in the 1930s. He designed and built houses in a variety of styles, taking work as it came to him from outside designers, and later incorporating those styles in his own work, including examples of Shingle/Craftsman and Colonial Revival. His building career came later than the development of the Boothbay area, and that fact is reflected in the relative absence of Queen Anne in his summer houses, and the relative abundance of hybridized Craftsman and Colonial Revival styles. (Queen Anne is well represented in Southwest Harbor, but not in Norwood's work.) The five houses presented here include two designed from architect's plans (one definitely, one nearly definitely), one built by Norwood from informal sketches provided by the owner, and two most likely designed by Norwood using designs wholly his own or using pattern book drawings as style guides.

Rachel Cope Evans Cottage, Southwest Harbor, Maine (R. M. Norwood, 1924), interior window lighting staircase. Enclosed interior spaces like stairwells and closets can be lit by adding windows that open onto another interior space. Here, double-hung sash windows were installed in a staircase landing to let in light from the kitchen and back porch.

Norwood's houses are also distinctive in being more substantially built than most summer houses and in being (in the cases of Norwood's own designs, at least) comparable in style to the many year-round houses of the same period in Southwest Harbor. His designs show less of the spur-of-the-moment spontaneity than the earlier houses at Squirrel Island, but Norwood was at the peak of his working years well after the end of the experimental period of the 1870s–1890s, a period when the very traditionally observant and historically oriented Colonial Revival was most firmly established in domestic architecture. His consistency may also reflect his comparatively large-scale operation, one requiring organization and delegation of responsibilities. Norwood's greatest strengths as a builder may have been his high

The BRENTWOOD (Size 34x26')

The Brentwood is a masterpiece in architecture. Its stately individuality causes it to stand alone in any community as a home of rare grace and permanent beauty; and yet so carefully have its designers considered economy in construction, that it is well within the means of those contemplating the erection of a home of its dimensions.

Catalog plan for The Brentwood (publisher source unknown, possibly the Aladdin Homes Co. of Bay City, Michigan), probably used as the model for the Hope Norwood Bannister House (collection of Susan W. Hodge). Norwood would not have used a precut or kit house, which were very popular at this time, but floor plans and elevations from the various architectural publications of the day were frequently used as conceptual documents, in the same way the plan catalogs such as those produced by Gustaf Stickley's Craftsman Architects were used.

level of craftsmanship, skill at execution of work within defined limits, and ability to consistently meet the desires and budgets of a wide range of clients.

HOPE NORWOOD BANNISTER HOUSE, SOUTHWEST HARBOR

Robie Norwood's daughter, Hope, was in college in 1925, when Norwood built this house for his family, a popular Colonial Revival style probably designed in part from a catalog plan. The family was living at the time at another location in Southwest Harbor, but Hope was to host a sorority party that year, and Norwood took the occasion as a motivation to complete a new house, suitable for the party. The house was ready in time and remains in the Norwood family today.

The overall style and plan of the house corresponds closely to a catalog picture kept by the family, although many interior features, such as special-use cabinets, are clearly his own design. The source of the catalog picture is unknown, but it appears to be contemporary with the house and was possibly a catalog advertisement for a precut house from one of the popular prefabricated housing manufacturers, such as

Colonial Revival (Dutch Colonial) house built for Norwood's daughter, Hope Norwood Bannister (R. M. Norwood, 1925).

Aladdin, Sears Roebuck, and Wardway (Montgomery Ward). Norwood would not have routinely erected a precut house (although he did do so on at least one occasion[18]). In the case of the Hope Norwood Bannister house, he probably used the single illustration from the catalog as a style guide but undertook all the design details himself.

There is abundant documentation[19] of American builders using catalog plans in ways other than those intended, most often by taking conceptual ideas from illustrations (or from actual houses built from plans) and producing their own drawings, thus sidestepping the fees charged for the full plans. The authors and publishers of plan books and mail-order architectural services loudly protested this "architectural piracy" and routinely copyrighted or patented drawings in an effort to ensure that one set of plans was sold for every house built. Still, the copying of design ideas was nearly impossible to prevent, especially when the derivatives went beyond simple copies and became extensions and even improvements on the published work. In the end, the architectural profession resigned itself to the leakage and adaptation of virtually all good ideas, and one journal even advised the offended authors to console themselves with the thought that, through their drawings, they were "moulding the vernacular architecture into shapes consistent with the higher civilization."[20]

The Hope Norwood Bannister house is not in any sense a "summer house"; it was built as a primary residence, was used throughout the year, and does not show the kind of free-form experimentation that marks many summer houses. It does, however, suggest the range of Norwood's skills and sense of design and gives some insight into the basis from which he worked when adapting designs, either of his own or those produced by others, to the specific needs and desires of summer residents.

Rachel Cope Evans Cottage, Manset

In the summer of 1924, Southwest Harbor summer visitor Rachel Cope Evans contracted with Robie Norwood to build a modest and unobtrusive cottage immediately on the water in the Manset part of Southwest Harbor. The house is simple and regular in shape, with two floors laid out under a single gable with shed dormers facing both land and water. There are a total of six bedrooms in this compact house but no servant's quarters. The surrounding forest – now, if not in 1924 – shields the house on all sides and makes the simple structure even more unobtrusive. Here, as will be seen in so many cases, the house is not an architectural or social statement to be viewed from outside, but rather a shelter and setting for the social life of the occupants in harmony with its environmental context: architecture for the people within.

Rachel Cope Evans evidently enjoyed the kind of trusting relationship for which Norwood was known. In a letter dated September 30, 1934, she relates to her children news of the house being planned at that time:

Rachel Cope Evans Cottage, Southwest Harbor, Maine (R. M. Norwood, 1924), exterior. The house sits within a few feet of the shoreline's winter berm and is closely surrounded by a screen of trees.

Rachel Cope Evans Cottage, Southwest Harbor, Maine (R. M. Norwood, 1924), Stickwork porch and rail.

A. is doing her best to see that the deed for the property is made out properly. . . . I hope we can arrange to have all marked out, as to road & house, before we leave, and then leave it to Mr. Norwood. . . .[21]

The silver-gray weathering characteristic of ocean-side environments is visible here; compare the color of these weathered white cedar shingles to that of weathered red cedar shingles at, for example, the Young Cottage in Randolph, New Hampshire, or the Bancroft Cottage at Caspian Lake, Vermont. The color differences of weathered shingles between coastal and inland sites are only partly due to the species of shingle used. White cedar shingles will normally darken more when used at inland sites than at coastal sites, while red cedar may darken less at coastal sites than inland. The color changes arise from two factors: ultraviolet degradation and the growth of fungal microorganisms, most commonly mildew (*Aureobasidium pullulans*). While the presence of salt in coastal environments has been suggested as a cause of the lighter, silver discoloration of coastal shingles (by inhibiting the growth of *A. pullulans*), the ultimate cause of the difference is unknown.

Rachel Cope Evans Cottage, Southwest Harbor, Maine (R. M. Norwood, 1924). Main room with fieldstone fireplace.

HALF ACRE (FRANK LEWIS COTTAGE), SOUTHWEST HARBOR

Norwood built this compact house in 1925 on a point near the center of Southwest Harbor during a period of summer cottage development in the 1920s and 1930s on land owned by, among others, descendants of Charles H. Fernald. The house is strongly influenced by the Craftsman style in its shingle cladding, deep gable eaves, and shed dormers, but it also shows Colonial Revival influences in its comparatively high profile (relative to a purely Craftsman design), and a street entrance portico with pediment.

The purpose of Half Acre as a summer home is evident in the interior, which is not insulated and has exposed, or open-stud, framing. The unfinished interior was not only a cost-saving measure in a house not occupied in winter but a historical reference to summer "camps" such as the nineteenth-century fishing camps at Rangeley Lakes, Maine, where rusticity was intrinsic, ubiquitous, and extremely influential on later, more deliberately styled designs. While no plans for this house are known to survive, Half Acre was likely built from a catalog plan with standard studding that was simply left unfinished, rather than designed specifically for an exposed-frame interior. Compare this house to the Will Bradley house (1906) or Dorothy Young house (1922), both in Randolph, New Hampshire (Chapter 5), where the structural framing was laid out and assembled to be the house's interior finish.

CONNER COVE (JOSEPH E. AND JANET BOOTH BROWN) COTTAGE, SOUTHWEST HARBOR

Ranged in a long, descending sweep toward the water, the Conner Cove Cottage mirrors its landscape on a point dropping into Somes Sound. This house was almost surely built from an architect's plan provided to Norwood by the house's owners, Joseph E. and Janet B. Brown, of Princeton, New Jersey. The house contrasts with the very simple Rachel Cope Evans Cottage, or the Hope Norwood Bannister and Frank Lewis Cottages – both built in established styles and probably from stock plans. The house plan is simple but large for a summer house (approximately 2,000 square feet). Viewed from the outside, it is dominated by steep, low rooflines and a towering fieldstone chimney. Inside, the rooflines contain a high-ceilinged, open-studded

Frank Lewis Cottage, Southwest Harbor, Maine (R. M. Norwood, 1923).

ABOVE LEFT: *Façade on ocean side of house, with Craftsman details, including shingle siding and diamond-pane windows, and more formal Colonial Revival-influenced porch details.*

ABOVE RIGHT: *Street entrance portico. The more formal Colonial Revival influence is most obvious here and in the porch details on the ocean side of this house.*

Frank Lewis Cottage, Southwest Harbor, Maine (R. M. Norwood, 1923).

ABOVE: *Main room, showing exposed studding.*

LEFT: *Porch interior on ocean side.*

main room with windows giving views through forest to the water. The extended (nearly eighty feet long) main axis of the house is of a scale consistent with its height, and placed on the wooded slope descending to the water, it keeps the house close to the ground and in harmony with its site.

The house – its shape and placement in the landscape, the height of its roof and chimney sweeping down to the ground and water – is dramatic. The Hope Bannister Norwood House, Norwood's own home, is conventional but solid, convivial, social, and in these ways consistent with Norwood's own role in the community. Half Acre is simplified, a standard but graceful design adapted in practical fashion for summer use. Rachel Cope Evans's house on the water is intimate, closely contained, quiet. Conner Cove Cottage hints at the exotic, some of the fancy of Squirrel Island, but with a heavier bearing and sense of attachment to the place, surely the intention of the owners and their architect, but also characteristic of Norwood's careful and methodical practices.

Conner Cove Cottage, Southwest Harbor, Maine (R. M. Norwood, architect unknown, 1923), exterior. The long roof lines and deep eaves create the house's sense of shelter and connection to the ground. The enormous chimney simultaneously reinforces the massive quality of the roof and, by thrusting a vertical line up through it, prevents the roof from being oppressive or confining.

Conner Cove Cottage, Southwest Harbor, Maine (R. M. Norwood, architect unknown, 1923).

ABOVE: *The site surrounding the cottage has been carefully pre-served, and a screen of trees partly shields the house from the open water of the cove.*

RIGHT: *Bedroom, with open-studded walls and an unusual ceiling treatment, with tongue-and-groove pine covering the ceiling rafters.*

Conner Cove Cottage, Southwest Harbor, Maine (R. M. Norwood, architect unknown, 1923), interior, main room. Several subtle features maintain a balance between the high roof and the living space below. The height of the room is emphasized by long vertical studs and rafters and roof cross-ties at a much higher level than a normal ceiling, but the effect of these lines is to expand the scale of the room below to match the roof. The large window and high stonework around the fireplace accomplish the same purpose. Skylights added after the original house construction light the large space above the cross ties and help to reduce dark voids above. Similar features appear, applied at much larger scales, in the lodge architecture (Old Faithful Inn at Yellowstone National Park, for example) used in National Park buildings designed in the early twentieth century.

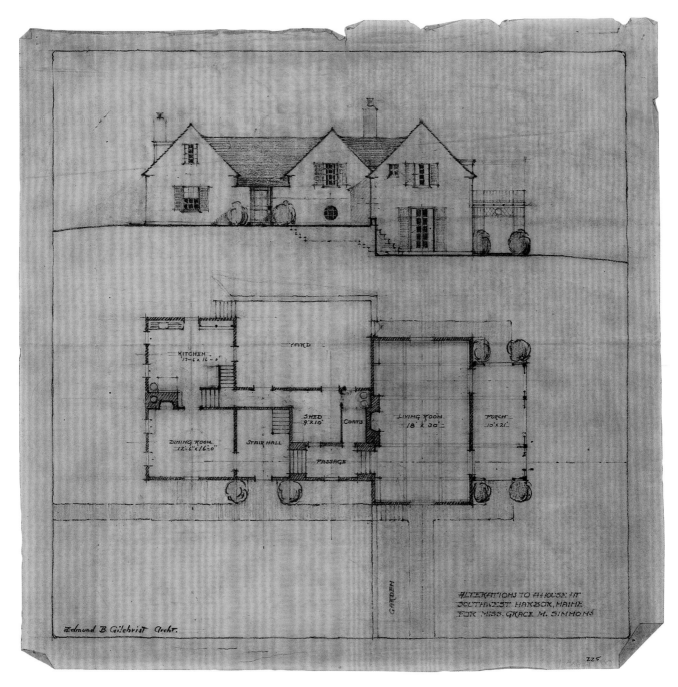

Elevation and ground floor plan of Grace Simmons House by architect Edmund B. Gilchrist (R. M. Norwood builder, 1922). (Edmund Beaman Gilchrist Collection, The Architectural Archives, University of Pennsylvania.)

John C. Harmon/Grace Simmons Cottage, Southwest Harbor

The original John C. Harmon house was built around 1860 and was remodeled for Grace Simmons by Robie Norwood in 1923 as a larger vacation house, following plans by architect Edmund B. Gilchrist of Philadelphia.

One of the most striking features of the alteration is the extension of the original front Cape Cod structure down the slope in an essentially split-level design, thirty years before the modern split-level house became a popular style and mainstay of U.S. domestic housing. The general character of the traditional Cape is preserved in the alteration, and dropping of levels by half-stories as the house descends a moderately steep slope keeps the apparent scale of the house consistent with the very small original building. The interior is plastered, more formal in character than a typical summer residence and, in fact, more formal than the original house.

John C. Harmon/Grace Simmons Cottage, Southwest Harbor (remodeled, E. B. Gilchrist architect, R. M. Norwood builder, 1922). View from ocean side.

John C. Harmon / Grace Simmons Cottage, Southwest Harbor (remodeled, E. B. Gilchrist architect, R. M. Norwood builder, 1922).

ABOVE LEFT: *Photograph of the Grace Simmons Cottage at the time of its remodeling in 1922, following Edmund B. Gilchrist's design. The draping of the house over the top of the hill is clear in this view. (Edmund Beaman Gilchrist Collection, The Architectural Archives, University of Pennsylvania.)*

ABOVE RIGHT: *Grace Simmons Cottage, 2005. Same view as the 1922 photograph.*

LEFT: *Two short staircases join the house's three parts, climbing a few steps between different ground-floor levels.*

John C. Harmon / Grace Simmons Cottage, Southwest Harbor (remodeled, E. B. Gilchrist architect, R. M. Norwood builder, 1922).

RIGHT: *Main door and staircase joining different ground-floor levels, view down toward the end of the house facing the ocean.*

BELOW: *Fireplace and paneling. This style of wall paneling was a defining element of Adam and Georgian interiors, and widespread in late-eighteenth- and early-nineteenth-century New England. This house probably never had such an elegant interior in its original form, however.*

INLAND MAINE

~~~~~~

RANGELEY LAKES REGION

UP RIVER, AWAY FROM Maine's rocky and convoluted coast, a traveler encounters a landscape opening into low, rolling hills, wide valleys holding fields and marshes, and hundreds of lakes. Far to the northwest the land is thrown up into steeper mountains covered with deep forest – the northernmost extension of the Appalachian Mountains, draped across the state from its border with New Hampshire to Mt. Katahdin. The greater part of the woods and mountains of western and northern Maine are wild and unpopulated today, cut only by logging roads to their northern extremity at the Canadian border and the edge of the great St. Lawrence Valley.

As remote as northwestern and northern Maine is today, one is tempted to suppose that it was always trackless wilderness up to the arrival of loggers in the late nineteenth century. But the early settlement of distant parts of New England was not a steady progression from the older centers of population. Following the end of the French and Indian War in 1763, settlers scattered sparsely but almost immediately across the entire region. Isolated farmsteads sprang up first in the last decades of the eighteenth century along the major rivers, and then incrementally, during the first decades of the nineteenth century, into the less accessible lands beyond and between the rivers. Not all of these settlements survived, especially after the westward expansion and migration of agriculture in the mid-1800s. Many parts of New England were more populated a century or more ago, and their countryside was more cultivated and tamed than today, as farms return to forest and as populations cluster in smaller numbers of larger towns. The Rangeley Lakes region, which over the past 150 years hosted tourists and fishermen at more than one hundred hotels and commercial camps located in or near the town of Rangeley, is one of these vanishing places. The big hotels have almost completely disappeared, as have many of the camps, and the pasture and croplands of a previous century are steadily returning to forest – a change toward a new wilderness rather than a carefully husbanded relict of the past.

In 1796, James Rangeley, in company with three other men, bought thirty thousand acres of lake country at the headwaters of the Androscoggin River from the Commonwealth of Massachusetts.[1] Rangeley and his company never occupied

Bonney Camp, Rangeley Lake, Maine, porch view through Adirondack-style stickwork. The heavily framed porch roof will support a substantial winter snow load.

Kennebago River at its entrance into Cupsuptic Lake, Rangeley Lakes, Maine.

their lands, however, and the lakes remained in sole possession of their ancestral occupants, the Abenaki Indians, for another two decades. The first European settlers arrived in 1816 or 1817, when Luther Hoar, accompanied by his wife and eight children, left their former home in Madrid, Maine, and arrived at the "Lake Settlement" on the eastern shore of what is now Rangeley Lake. In the next few years Hoar was joined by several other families, including those of John Toothaker and David Quimby – all names which can be found today not only attached to places, such as Toothaker Island, but also among the area's present residents, descendants of the original settlers. Rangeley never saw his land, but his son, James Rangeley Jr., inherited his father's share and later bought out the other three partners. In 1825 he moved himself and his family onto the land with plans to build a community and economy based on agriculture, lumber, and mining. The younger Rangeley's discovery of Hoar's settlement on his land, already established as a modest community engaged in farming and logging, fit his ambitions nicely, and rather than eject the squatters, Rangeley welcomed them and adapted his plan to their presence.

Five big lakes and a constellation of smaller lakes and ponds form the Androscoggin headwaters, which rise in a high plateau close up against the crest of the northern Appalachians. Two of the big lakes still bear their original Indian names, Mooselookmeguntic and Cupsuptic, but the three others, Oquossoc, Mollychunkamunk, and Welokennabacook, are now better known as Rangeley Lake, and Upper and Lower Richardson Lakes. The big lakes had been rich hunting and fishing grounds for the Abenaki for generations, and the new settlers quickly discovered that fish, especially brook trout, thrived in the clear, cold waters of the lakes. Even despite their remoteness, by the 1840s a few sport fishermen were coming from Rhode Island, Connecticut,[2] and New York to explore the lakes and investigate their angling potential. By this time the "Lake Settlement" on Oquossuc Lake was known as the town of Rangeley and had grown to thirty-nine families. Logging was also on the rise, with the Androscoggin River filled with logs destined for sawmills downstream. The river itself was beginning its long career as one of New England's industrial arteries, initially a corridor for transportation of logs and a source of hydroelectric power, and later a conduit and repository for the waste of the pulp and paper industry. One of the first stages in that evolution was the construction in 1850 of the Upper Dam at the western end of Mooselookmeguntic Lake. This dam was used to raise the water levels in the lake, linking it to Cupsuptic Lake and facilitating the movement of logs. As a side benefit, the dam created pools and spillways that made especially good fish habitats and increased the sport-fishing potential of the place even further.

In 1860, Henry O. Stanley (Maine's fisheries commissioner after 1883) and

Measles, *Rangeley Boat, Frank Barrett, 1928.*

New Yorker George S. Page visited Rangeley to investigate the rumors of good fishing. They discovered, as claimed, large and abundant brook trout in the big lakes. Page returned to New York with eight trout, ranging between five and eight pounds,[3] packed in sawdust and ice (getting fresh fish from the wilds of Maine to New York City was presumably no small trick in 1860). Their adventure drew public attention to the Rangeley Lakes, and their report of the quality and size of the fish was met with some incredulity by sportsmen back in the city. Skeptics were satisfied with Stanley and Page's story only after Harvard naturalist Louis Agassiz inspected Page's catch and confirmed that the fish were indeed brook trout and not lake trout or some other less desirable species.[4] Fish – not just plentiful fish but *big* fish, with trophy potential – started to make Rangeley famous at roughly the same time that the recreational potential of the Adirondack Mountains was attracting notice. The quality of sport fishing in the Rangeley region compared favorably with that in the Adirondacks, and soon many of the residents of Rangeley began to supplement farming and logging by the more profitable, easier, and probably more fun occupation of guiding.

From the 1870s on, Rangeley built its fortunes around recreational fishing, although logging especially continued to be a major economic force in northwestern Maine, bringing in roads and railroads which served tourists in addition to industry. Guidebooks[5] described the geography of the lakes and mountains, gave advice on securing guides' services, and provided details on transportation by rail, road, and steamboat, as well as on accommodations at the rapidly increasing number of hotels and commercial camps catering principally to fishermen – and, as it turned out, fisherwomen. Fly fishing, rather than live bait or cast lures, was the fishing style of choice at Rangeley, and no one in the last decades of the nineteenth century devoted greater energy to the promotion of fly fishing, the Rangeley Lakes, and Maine in general as a sporting destination than Cornelia T. "Fly Rod" Crosby (1854–1946).[6] Crosby's accomplishments as a writer and personality were part of a larger effort conducted by a number of individuals, businesses, and state agencies to boost Maine's economy through tourism at a time when the state's agricultural strength was declining due to westward emigration, and its manufacturing industries were facing ever-increasing competition from southern New England mill towns. In 1895, long before "Vacationland" appeared on Maine motor vehicle license plates (that happened in 1936), the Maine Sportsman's Fish and Game Association urged legislators' attention by claiming that hunting, fishing, and related support services constituted the state's most important source of income.[7] Whether the Association's claim was correct or not, they acted as an extremely effective lobbying organization for all businesses with an interest in tourism (including, significantly, the Maine Central Railroad) and heavily influenced commercial development in Maine as a tourist destination. The Association also pressed for legislation establishing fish and game regulations, typically to benefit the out-of-state visitors, or "sports," who came for the hunting and fishing.

Fly Rod herself stayed away from such controversial issues as the effects of seasonal closures and bag limits on local subsistence hunters and fishers, but she consistently urged the need for conservation and was an early advocate of catch-and-release fishing. Strong conservation efforts were needed, for even Rangeley's legendary population of giant brook trout couldn't survive the pressure of the hundreds of "sports" who arrived at Rangeley after Maine's exhibit (designed and managed mostly by Crosby) in the 1895 Sportsman's Exhibition in New York City. In the early days, fishermen gloried not only in catching big fish, but also in catching *many* fish: one skilled fly caster could potentially catch hundreds of fish in a day, the vast majority of which would be discarded in the woods along the shoreline. The brook trout population also suffered from competition with landlocked salmon, introduced for sport fishing in 1875 and a voracious eater of blueback trout (*Salvelinus aureolus oquassa*), the brook trout's principal forage and source of its great size. Despite the guides' and clients' gradual adoption of catch-and-release fishing, the really big trout eventually vanished, but the fishing remained formidable. It put Rangeley on the map and created a summer destination and camp architecture built not around idle leisure, high society, or intellectual contemplation, but around rough-and-ready sport.

The fishing camps are Rangeley's unique architectural contribution. Originating in the simplest concepts of shelter – roof and hearth – the Rangeley fishing camps became something more than rustic cabins by virtue of their shared use, either by

Camp Kennebago, Rangeley Lakes, Maine. (Maine Historic Preservation Commission.)

ABOVE LEFT: *Exterior view, circa 1873–78. The Oquossuc Angling Association was founded in 1868 by New Yorker George Page and several other East Coast fishing enthusiasts. The OAA was instrumental in the development of Rangeley as a sport-fishing destination, as well as in early conservation and game management efforts.*

ABOVE RIGHT: *Dormitory in main building, circa. 1873–78.*

Camp Kennebago, Rangeley Lakes, Maine.

paying clients or by members of a private club who shared in a camp's use and ownership. The first private fishing club in the Rangeley region, the Oquossuc Angling Association, was founded in 1868 by George S. Page and several fellow fishing enthusiasts. Page and his colleagues bought a substantial parcel of land on Cupsuptic Lake, where they built their headquarters and base of operations. Camp Kennebago was designed for shared use by the Association's members and consisted of a large dormitory sleeping room and adjacent kitchen and dining area, all contained in a rectangular space some one hundred feet long by thirty feet wide and open to the ridge of a single gable roof. The interior space was minimally divided – the single dormitory contained at least the thirteen beds visible in one photograph – and was entirely unfinished. Privacy was neither expected nor desired.[8] An adjacent building provided separate rooms for married couples, and eventually private cabins were added for members with families. The need to provide services to clients efficiently required some compartmentalization of space by use, for example into service, kitchen, and dining areas, but these needs were met without completely isolating those spaces as they might be in a conventional hotel.[9] Communal spaces shared by loosely connected acquaintances linked by a common interest in fishing created an atmosphere of informal collegiality and reinforced the rustic nature of their activity and setting. The fact that the guests at Camp Kennebago were clients paying for a well-orchestrated experience did not alter its authenticity;

the services and accommodations provided were simple, comfortable without being indulgent, and appropriate for the place and purpose. Buildings were deliberately functional, often built for use and occupancy by large numbers, either members of a club or an extended family. Activities like dining, sleeping, and socializing would often have separate structures. The origins of this style of architecture, what Harvey Kaiser[10] calls a "compound plan," are unknown but became common, particularly in lake settings, across northern New England.

The Rangeley camps were distinguished from their more or less contemporaneous Adirondack counterparts by their consistently utilitarian function. The Adirondack Lodge style had very similar origins, but those origins were quickly eclipsed by the "Great Camps," which took the basic functionality of the fishing camp and transformed it into a social and aesthetic display not unlike the "cottages" of Newport and Bar Harbor. By retaining their simple style and construction, the Rangeley camps continued to embody the most essential elements of shelter, physical and emotional communication with the environment, and communal experience of nature. Ultimately becoming iconic representations of robust outdoor living, they were used (at Squam Lake in New Hampshire, in 1881) as prototypes for summer youth camp architecture.[11]

Fishing wasn't the only activity that made Rangeley the destination it became in its boom years, for the lakes also offered health resorts and vacation hotels oriented, unlike the camps, more toward leisure than sport. Between 1860 and World War II, more than a hundred hotels, clubs, and commercial camps operated on the

Camp Kemankeag, Rangeley Lake, Maine, main house. This is the original building in this camp, built around 1890 for the Farmington (Maine) Fishing Club. The house is unusual in having two parallel gables, but is otherwise typical of local vernacular buildings from a slightly earlier period. White clapboard siding and shelf returns on the eaves show the persistent, if vestigial, influence of the Greek Revival so common across northern New England. To the left of the main building, two more houses, identical to each other, can be seen. These were built in 1922 to the design of a subsequent owner; one, with a single main room downstairs and bedrooms upstairs, housed adults, while the other, with a single large dormitory bedroom upstairs and smaller rooms below, housed the family's children.

Camp Kemankeag, Rangeley Lake, Maine.

ABOVE: *Main house kitchen and dining room. Originally partitions divided this space into kitchen, pantry, dining room, and maid's quarters. This was later opened into a long single space combining cooking and dining areas. The interior finish of this camp has the rough and informal nature characteristic of its original purpose as a jointly owned fishing club.*

LEFT: *Main house, staircase.*

Camp Kemankeag, Rangeley Lake, Maine. Upstairs corridor joining bedrooms. The simple fishing camp interior is even simpler here on the second floor, where camps and cottages normally used rougher lumber and fewer finish details.

shores of the big lakes. The large establishments – hotels of one hundred rooms and more, virtually all gone today – were beautiful buildings, but, beyond their remote setting, not different in any large degree from other grand resort hotels elsewhere in New England. Many of the individual cottages that surrounded the hotels, most built as annexes to the hotels themselves and integral to the hotel property, have survived and are now in private ownership.

These surviving hotel cottages share many of the qualities of summer houses described on the Maine coast; the fishing camps less so. A working distinction between "camp" and "cottage" can be seen here[12]: camps are the product of a building up of primitive units of shelter and hearth, possibly through an intermediate tent phase, to create a domestic dwelling for simplified or occasional use, while cottages are a scaling down of traditional or "conventional" domestic architecture (as Down-

RIGHT: *Mingo Springs Hotel,*
Mingo Springs Resort, Rangeley,
Maine.

BELOW RIGHT: *Belcher Camp,*
Rangeley, Maine, main room.
Framing is exposed in the interior
of the Belcher Camp, with the
purlin-and-rafter system support-
ing the ceiling, as seen in several
other camps and cottages through-
out northern New England. The
stud walls are sheathed on one
side in beadboard
tongue-and-groove.

The Bungalows—Mingo Spring House and Camps—Rangeley Lake, Maine

ing advocated) for essentially the same purpose. The hotel cottages at Rangeley, and the summer houses of coastal Maine described earlier largely fall into the "cottage" category (although some, such as Norwood's houses at Southwest Harbor, are arguably too large and too standard in construction to be classified as cottages), while the Rangeley fishing camps are virtually archetypes of the camp style. Ultimately both types serve the same purpose, and at a certain point the differences vanish and the distinction becomes academic. Comparing the interiors of the Camp Kemankeag (originally a fishing camp) to the Bonney or Belcher Camps (cottages by this definition),

Belcher Camp, Rangeley, Maine.

ABOVE: *Originally part of the Mingo Springs Resort, the Belcher Camp is now privately owned. Several companion camps, visible in the postcard view, are now gone, and the boardwalk, mowed lawns, and generally manicured surroundings shown in the postcard have grown back up into trees; the camp itself is relatively unchanged. The basic plan and massing of the house is a simple gable-end unit with an added T wing, but decorative details such as the exposed rafter ends, hipped roof on the wing, and transition from clapboard to shingles at the second-floor level show Craftsman / Bungalow influences. The clapboard-to-shingle transition is also visible in the postcard view from sometime before 1920. Note that the Adirondack-style stickwork porch posts and rail are a modern addition; in the postcard view, the porch is supported by square posts with modest scroll-sawn decorative trim.*

LEFT: *Second floor door and corridor. With no building codes governing details like minimum corridor widths, staircase pitch, or staircase landing areas, small camps and cottages tended to have very cramped and irregular upstairs corridors to maximize the size of the rooms. The board-and-batten door shown here is also typical of the simpler and more rustic style in which upper floors were finished.*

Bonney Camp, Rangeley Lake, Maine. The exterior of the Bonney Camp is very similar in style to the Belcher Camp, although it was not a part of the Mingo Springs Resort. Note the decorative clapboard-to-shingle transition at the second floor and Adirondack-style stickwork porch (again, as at the Belcher Camp, quite possibly a later addition).

differences in style, construction, and finish can be seen, but a meaningful distinction becomes very fine indeed.

As Rangeley's status as a commercial resort destination declined during and following World War II, its camps and cottages started to pass into private hands. The clustered, multiple-structure style of the fishing camps lent itself well to occupancy by extended families and multiple generations. Here, as in so many summer communities, the camp or cottage often became the annual meeting place for extended families scattered geographically and across generations. Frequently the family camp became the true "home," the one fixed and unvarying place where grandparents, children, and grandchildren shared not only a common experience, but to a large degree a common identity as each passed through childhood, adolescence, and adulthood, in a place far less variable and evolving than what was experienced in the "real" world of careers and modern life.

Bonney Camp, Rangeley Lake, Maine,

ABOVE: *Bathhouse. This combined laundry and bathroom occupies a completely separate structure adjacent to the main house. The pressure tank on the left is a typical component of surface- or lake-water collection systems where (like a drilled well) the house water pressure must be maintained by pressurizing a small reservoir held in the tank.*

LEFT: *Main room. "On the far wall of the barn, a school of paper fish swam among the racing pennants that lay like eelgrass on the rough pine walls. They were the traced silhouettes of memorable catches made by my aunts and uncles decades earlier, carefully cut from white blotting paper and inscribed with India ink with the particulars of their demise." – George Howe Colt,* The Big House

BELGRADE LAKES REGION

*Androscoggin River near Maine–
New Hampshire border.*

After fly rods were packed and fish mounted, iced, or eaten, Rangeley's sports would return to civilization not in company with the logs floating down the Androscoggin, but by a variety of routes, traveling overland by wagon and railroad. One route ran southeast, following the Sandy River to Phillips, Fly Rod Crosby's home. From Phillips, the Sandy River Railroad ran to Farmington, and from there the Maine Central Railroad continued down and across the Kennebec valley to Portland and points south. Along the route toward the Kennebec, the Sandy River meanders between low hills and then into pastures and rich river-bottom crop land, cleared late in the eighteenth century as the state's first inland farming settlements were established. Along the way, tucked up close against the Kennebec River near Waterville, are the seven lakes comprising the Belgrade Lakes region (Long, Great, Messalonskee, North, East, McGraw, and Ellis), and among them, the town of Belgrade, first settled in 1774 and incorporated as Belgrade in 1796.

Belgrade, like any rural inland settlement in early New England, was by necessity built around farming. As well as soil, however, the town of Belgrade had a valuable resource in the water power available through its lakes. In the early years of the nineteenth century, enterprising residents built sawmills and gristmills, and by mid-century they had expanded their industries with water-powered factories producing farm tools and wood products, including shingles, spools, and excelsior packing material. Belgrade at that time reflected the state's economic rise in microcosm. Maine's greatest wealth lay in fish, trees, and water, for the industries that built Maine through most of the nineteenth century included commercial fishing, boat-building, logging, and water-powered manufacture along its big rivers. The state's fortunes didn't improve unchecked, however, for eventually the railroad – the same technology that had "boomed" Maine during the rise of lumber and sporting tourism – started having an opposite influence, carrying farmers away to new and better lands in the Midwest, and bringing in food and manufactured items that competed with local production. Maine's national dominance of the logging and fishing industries in the 1860s shrank drastically in the next four decades, while manufacturing held on longer but eventually lost ground to centrally located competitors in southern New England and elsewhere. At the end of the nineteenth century, faced with losses of their traditional industries, towns across Maine commonly responded by shifting – as Rangeley had in the 1860s when woodland guiding provided an opportunity – toward tourism and service-related occupations.

Limited tourist-oriented businesses probably operated at a low level in Belgrade for many years, only growing to significant size when the rest of the state followed the model Fly Rod Crosby had initiated and established at Rangeley in the late

Great Pond, Belgrade Lakes, Maine.

1890s. Crosby was nominally an advocate for fishing and sporting tourism across all of Maine, but the Rangeley Lakes district was her home territory, and her partiality for the place showed in her writings and the promotional displays at sporting exhibitions in New York, Boston, and in Maine. Following the 1895 Sportsman's Exposition in New York, Crosby's focus on Rangeley began to draw criticism from guides and commercial interests in other parts of the state. Ever the diplomat, Crosby responded by expanding her scope of travel and reporting and visiting fishing destinations at Moosehead Lake, Aroostook County, and, by 1902, the Belgrade Lakes. These events also coincided with the passage of the Maine Guide's bill in 1897, which formalized the training and licensing of "Maine Guides" (of whom Crosby was the first) and reinforced the state's commercial interest in sporting tourism.

Belgrade Hotel, Belgrade Lakes, Maine (John Calvin Stevens, 1899).

Of Belgrade's several successful hotels, the first was Belgrade Hotel (1899), designed by John Calvin Stevens. Around the same time, the first tourist camp opened, Cornelius Kelliher's Winona Beach Camp.[13] However, Belgrade's place in fishing and tourism must have extended back considerably before this time: an account of a fishing trip to Belgrade was published in 1831,[14] and the lakes were stocked with bass for sport fishing in 1875 and with salmon in 1878, only three years after Rangeley.

The principal camp-building period in the Belgrade Lakes region was in the early decades of the twentieth century, after the state's concerted effort to market its recreational potential. Although the town itself probably had some years of experience in tourism,[15] the origins of the Belgrade camp community and of the camp buildings themselves are uncertain. The hotel business flourished at Belgrade up through the 1920s but suffered (as did tourist destinations everywhere) in the period between 1929 and the end of World War II. Commercial camps like Kelliher's Winona Beach Camp seem not to have been as numerous as their cousins at Rangeley, and there is no clear evidence of commercial camps at Belgrade (either annexed to the hotels or operating independently) converting to private use. Individuals and families familiar with Belgrade's attractions from stays at the hotels may simply have bought land and started building their own camps. If the growth pattern is consistent with other communities, private camps appeared sometime during the height of the hotel era, typically with a further shift toward camps as the expense of extended hotel stays increased.

As at Rangeley, camps along the lakeshore were originally approached by water rather than road, and the majority of camps were placed very close to and facing the water. Boathouses built partly into the water were common and sometimes had living quarters included in them as well.

Another distinctive feature of the Belgrade camp's orientation toward water is the delivery of mail by water at Great Pond, the largest of the Belgrade Lakes. One of only four water postal routes in the U.S. (another is at New Hampshire's Lake Winnipesaukee), the century-old Great Pond mail route circles the lake daily in the summer months, a unique symbol of Belgrade's identity and a tangible link with its past.

Wilder Camp/Karonoko

Charles Wheeler Wilder was an architect from New Rochelle, New York, and a partner in the firm Barnard and Wilder. In 1901, very early in Belgrade's development as a summer destination, Wilder and his family first summered in tents on Great Pond. After purchasing property on Great Pond, Wilder built a group of camp buildings in a compound plan, which over the next twenty-four years he expanded to include sleeping quarters, social room, kitchen/dining room, guesthouses, an ice

Karonoko, Great Pond, Belgrade Lakes, Maine.

Karonoko, Great Pond, Belgrade Lakes, Maine.

LEFT: *Boathouse. For the protection of lake shorelines, new boathouses placed at the water's edge are no longer allowed at the Belgrade Lakes. Existing boathouses, such as Karonoko's, may remain.*

MIDDLE: *Main house.*

BELOW: *Sleeping house.*

RIGHT: *Karonoko, Great Pond, Belgrade Lakes, Maine. Sleeping house in compound plan.*

BELOW: *Sleeping house in compound plan, Great Pond, Belgrade, Maine.*

Karonoko, Great Pond, Belgrade Lakes, Maine, dining room interior.

house, and a shed. The main buildings, containing the social room and kitchen/dining room were linked by a covered walkway and porches that expanded the social areas. Guesthouses provided privacy with bedrooms and small social/sitting areas. All were placed very near the lake's edge and the boathouse, which included a small sleeping quarters in an upper story. Subsequent owners (the property was sold to a cousin of Wilder's in 1925) added a boathouse, maid's quarters, and other outbuildings. The second owners gave the camp complex a name, Karonoko, an amalgam of their children's names.

The styles of even the original buildings are harmonious but not identical, suggesting that they were constructed over some period of time. The connected social/

dining/kitchen group consists of one very simple gable-end building with very narrow eaves and brick chimney, and a slightly more complex hipped-roof building with much larger eaves, surrounding porches, exposed rafter ends, and fieldstone chimney. The covered walkways are decorated in simple Adirondack-style stickwork.

Compare the diversity of Karonoko's style with undated plans drawn by Wilder for a very similar camp ("Design for Bungalow, Belgrade Lakes, Maine"). In his drawings, Wilder unifies the compound-plan social/dining/kitchen units under a nearly continuous roofline carried between the separate buildings by the covered walkways, and develops the Adirondack-style stickwork more completely than at Karonoko. The general plan of Karonoko is preserved, and even the two roofs, gabled and hipped, are here, although reversed, with the simple gable covering the dining/cooking building. Despite the similarities, this plan is clearly not the plan for Karonoko. Given the diverse and apparently evolved style of Karonoko, the drawings are probably a refinement and consolidation of ideas developed piecemeal there, rather than a preexisting plan from which Karonoko diverged.

Wilder's arrival at a unified concept of the compound plan though his own experience building his family camp suggests that the compound plan was not well-known to him before 1901, or at least that he had not carefully articulated it architecturally. The compound plan was very popular at Belgrade Lakes, but Wilder's was one of the earliest of them, and in getting to formal designs he may have relied mostly on examples from the Adirondack "Great Camps" for guidance.[16]

Whatever the origins of the compound plan, it became a very widely used design concept, not only at Belgrade Lakes but at summer colonies (and, somewhat inexplicably, at lake locations especially) elsewhere in New England, and at youth

"Plan for Bungalow, Belgrade Lakes, Maine," plot layout (detail). Barnard and Wilder, New Rochelle, New York.

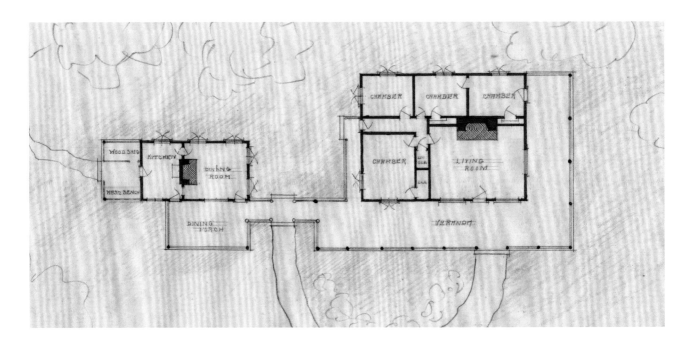

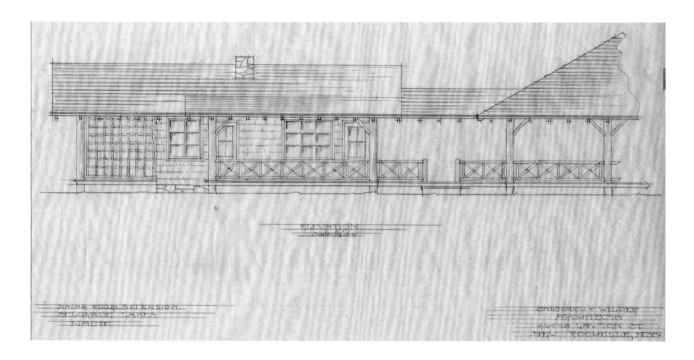

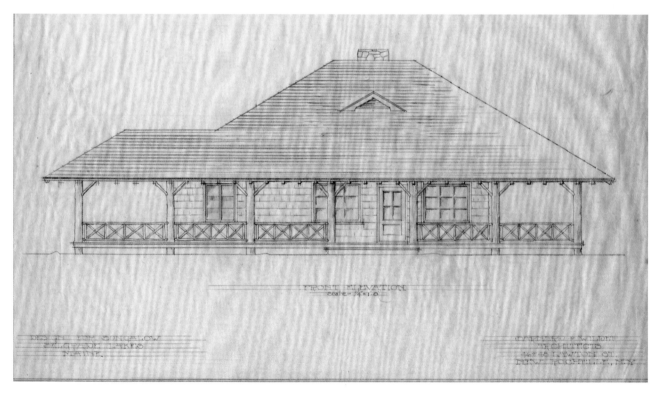

TOP: *"Plan for Bungalow, Belgrade Lakes, Maine," front elevation. Barnard and Wilder, New Rochelle, New York.*

ABOVE: *"Plan for Bungalow, Belgrade Lakes, Maine," dining room extension. Barnard and Wilder, New Rochelle, New York.*

camps (the earliest youth camp at Belgrade, Camp Merryweather, opened in 1900, only a year before Wilder came to Great Pond), where the compound plan worked very efficiently for large numbers of residents.

Why build a group of buildings to accommodate people and activities that were normally contained within a single structure, probably at lower expense? The privacy afforded by isolated buildings is one clear characteristic of the compound plan, but the social spirit of most summer communities at this time tended toward a sacrifice of privacy in favor of a shared social experience (expressed, for example, in Ripley Hitchcock's comments about Camp Kennebago in Rangeley). Fire protection is often given as a practical motivation for separating structures and was probably seen as an advantage of the compound plan if not its primary purpose.[17] In many of the lakeside examples at Belgrade, and elsewhere, however, the structures are placed so close together that the potential benefit in a fire is questionable. It seems most likely that the compound plan, whatever its origins may have been, grew in popularity principally as a desirable style, one that, once again, reinforced the connection between domesticity and wilderness, shelter and environment.

Camp Liberty, Great Pond, Belgrade Lakes, Maine. Camp Liberty's main structure consists of an elongated gable roof over a single story with a small T on the back containing a kitchen. Other detached buildings behind the main house provide additional space. The porch, running the length of the house and continuous with the main roof (rather than attaching to the wall beneath the main roof eave), is reminiscent of Mississippi Valley French Colonial architecture, one of the historical prototypes of the Bungalow.

Camp Liberty, Great Pond, Belgrade Lakes, Maine.

ABOVE: *Main room. Here the camp's framing is covered in beadboard with minimal disruption by trim. The continuous windows facing the lake slide in wooden tracks to open. The open partition in the foreground may have been remodeled from an earlier complete partition. Note breaks at the ends of the beadboard strip immediately above the central header; cuts like these are evidence of later alteration.*

LEFT: *Boathouse. Boathouses, perhaps more than any other building or architectural feature, symbolize summer life on the inland lakes.*

*Details from camps at Great
Pond, Belgrade Lakes, Maine.*

ABOVE: *Interior, boathouse. The
boathouse foundation rests on the
lake bottom at the shoreline and is
open on the end facing the water
to allow a boat to be pulled in.*

RIGHT: *Revolving table. Belgrade
fishing guide Bert Curtis served
his "signature fish chowder by use
of a revolving table" (John Mundt,
"Gilded Summers in Belgrade,
Maine" in* American Fly Fisher,
*2000). No definite connection is
known between Curtis's revolving
table and this one, but it is hard
to imagine that revolving tables
were particularly abundant in the
Belgrade Lakes.*

Details from camps at Great Pond, Belgrade Lakes, Maine.

TOP: *This log-sided camp, with surrounding porch on two sides, contains one very large room with a small kitchen at the rear of the building. Other adjacent buildings provide bedrooms and other spaces.*

ABOVE: *Another example of "Compound Plan" architecture, with different household functions accommodated in separate buildings.*

RIGHT: *Dining room.*

Details from camps at Great Pond, Belgrade Lakes, Maine.

ABOVE: *Sleeping house interior.*

RIGHT: *Sleeping house with shuttered screen walls. The exterior shutters are in two pieces, one hinged at the top and closing down over the upper third of the screen, and one hinged at the bottom and closing up from the lower sill. When open, the upper shutters form an awning over the window.*

NEW HAMPSHIRE

Departing from Boston and heading north, I avoided the main interstate highway and instead took the "old road" along the eastern border of New Hampshire, driving through Portsmouth, Dover, and eventually Chocorua and Conway. Once the growing sprawl of the south was finally behind me, I came into the rolling hills of the Lakes Region, the horizon hazy and close in the summer evening sun, the air thick with the day's heat and noisy with insects. State Route 16 led me through the Ossipees and along the shore of Lake Chocorua. Turning off the main road onto Fowler's Mill Road, I stopped on the tiny bridge which crosses a gap separating two parts of the lake. Looking across the lake from the bridge, the summit of Mount Chocorua stood close above the water, blazing on one side in the sunset and felt-blue in the shadows on the other. The air around me moved lightly, bearing with it an increasing silence as night approached.

I took one photograph and stood briefly looking over the hills of the Sandwich Range to the clouds behind, built in the heat of the day over the more distant Presidential Range and now shrinking, reabsorbed into the darkening purple sky as the sun set.

Continuing north, I passed through North Conway and Jackson and entered Pinkham Notch at dusk. I wound my way up through the mountains, the forest silent now, with a wind pushing out of the ravines and down the notch. Pinkham Notch divides the drainage of the Ellis River, flowing south, back down into the softer, rolling country of the Saco valley, from the Peabody River, flowing north to the harder, colder, and more isolated forests and mountains of Coos County. The warm, almost watery comfort of the countryside I had passed through a few hours before was behind me, and in its place was a sharp-edged clarity, the sound of the wind mixing with the falls on the Ellis River, and the stars over Mt. Washington bright over the horizon high above.

THE STATE OF New Hampshire today is known for its high mountains, deep forests, and broad lakes. Its seventeenth-century origins, though, lay in its scant eighteen miles of coast, wedged in between the far larger coasts of the colonies of Massachusetts Bay and Maine. Originally included as part of the colony of Maine, chartered in 1622, New Hampshire was extracted from Maine and established as a separate colony in 1629, defined as the coastline between the Merrimack and Piscataqua

Will H. Bradley house (1906), wall detail.

109

Rivers. In those very early days, the western horizon of European settlement in New England lay nearly within sight of the Atlantic coast, the interior being still the exclusive province of Indians, terra incognita to the English newcomers. New Hampshire's first settlement, Pannaway Plantation, was established in 1623 as a fort and fish processing station at present-day Rye, near Portsmouth and adjacent to the mouth of the Piscataqua River. The state's second settlement, Strawberry Banke, was founded at the site of present-day Portsmouth a few years later, and by 1640 additional settlements (peopled in part by refugees from the religious oligarchy in Massachusetts Bay) had been built at Exeter and within the "Upper Plantation" at the sites of the modern towns of Dover, Durham, and Stratham, all within about fifteen miles of the ocean. In its earliest days the colony was tied, economically and geographically, to the sea. New Hampshire's forests were known only at their outermost fringe, while the presence of the White Mountains was only hinted at, told of in Indian legends and visible in autumn and winter from the sea as distant snow-capped ramparts, shining in the northwest at sunrise.

The rivers were the earliest routes into the wilderness, followed cautiously and methodically at first[1] but more boldly once the English Crown turned to northern New England's forests as its primary source of ship's masts in 1653. Logs were already a critical part of the region's economy (New England's first sawmill was built at York, Maine, in 1623). The great white pines that filled the woods of Maine and New Hampshire yielded straight, sound trunks used for framing timbers and boards, but also often reached the required size, a minimum of twenty-four inches in diameter at the butt, to be used as masts for England's navy. Bringing the logs undamaged and in one piece to the coast for shipment to England was a major engineering and logistical challenge, solved in part by early "mast roads," which penetrated the wilderness away from the rivers and provided comparatively straight and level routes along which to move the tremendous trunks, some forty inches in diameter and 120 feet in length.

Logging of the forests of Maine and New Hampshire accelerated throughout the middle decades of the seventeenth century, and by the 1680s energetic and entrepreneurial lumbermen had become so profligate that the Crown was obliged to impose restrictions on cutting in the forests if their only source of masts was to be preserved. King James II appointed a surveyor general in 1685, responsible for the conduct of surveys to inventory and mark, by a "Broad Arrow" blaze on the trunk, trees to be reserved strictly for the Crown's use. The "Broad Arrow" laws remained in effect until 1776, when England's authority on this and all other matters was swept away by the Declaration of Independence.

The inland penetration of European settlement along the rivers and mast roads was to be short-lived, however, since the hostilities between settlers and Indians (as well as among Indian tribes), originating in the first days of the Plymouth Colony and substantially amplified by King Phillip's War in 1675, continued to fester over the next century. The animosities and prejudices established in those years inhibited settlement outside well-fortified coastal towns and were the beginnings of the cultural and territorial hostilities that exacerbated the French and Indian War a century later, during which New England's northern interior was virtually uninhabitable by Europeans. Only after the Treaty of Paris in 1763, in which France surrendered to Britain its claims – virtually all of North America east of the Mississippi – did the interior of New England become hospitable to settlers, and enterprising individuals and families, first English and later Scotch and Irish, quickly moved up the rivers and fanned out across the countryside.

SQUAM LAKE

The upstream course of the Merrimack River, after wandering west across Massachusetts some thirty miles, veers north and into New Hampshire's Lakes region. The Pemigewasset River, flowing south out of the very heart of the White Mountains, passes Lake Winnipesaukee on its west side and joins the Merrimack north of the state capital at Concord. The two rivers together with the other tributaries joining them comprise one of the great river systems of the northeast, both for the native populations and for the settlers who followed them. The rivers were arteries of transportation, and their valleys were home to Abenaki and Pennacook Indians and their ancestors going back to prehistoric times.[2] For the Europeans who followed, the Merrimack was a source of power as well as transportation and, during the nineteenth century, was among the most highly developed rivers in the world for water-powered manufacture. Farther upriver, though, the Pemigewasset meandered, mostly undisturbed by the industrial revolution, through its broad valley. At the present site of Holderness, the original town of New Holderness was settled in 1763 and grew through the next century principally as a farming and fishing community. One cascade at the confluence of the Squam and Pemigewasset Rivers was the site of a mill and, by 1868, became the town of Ashland, split off from Holderness and reached by railroad from the south. The rails carried the products of the mills south and eventually, as they had to Rangeley, brought tourists north.

Immediately to the northwest of the much larger Lake Winnipesauke, Squam Lake covers about 7,000 acres of open water fringed by a sprawling complex of peninsulas and coves. In the lake are scores of islands, some with houses on them but many so small that they are no more than isolated, water-lapped clusters of trees and rock. The shores of the lake were cleared for farming, as were most of the rolling lowlands of the river valleys, not long after its settlement in the late eighteenth century. By the mid-nineteenth century the place was an ideal location for summer travelers in search of a quiet, pastoral retreat. The lake, the nearby rolling hills and higher mountains of the Sandwich Range, and beyond them the summits of the loftier Presidential Range, combined the attractions of water and mountains in a location beyond the burgeoning commercial and industrial development farther south along the river. By the 1880s, private camps were appearing among the trees along the lakeshore and on the islands.

Summer camps on Squam Lake originated in one truly rustic camp, built from lumber scraps at Piper Cove in 1879. Camp Nirvana, built by three young men, Dartmouth College students Henry Burke Closson and Charles Merrill Hough, and a local resident, identified today only as "the Terry boy," was a camp in its purest sense: a primitive lean-to structure providing shelter from rain, a spot for a fire, and little else. For the three intrepid builders and their friends who joined them, how-

Sandwich Bay, Squam Lake, New Hampshire.

ever, it really was Nirvana, a state of being where all needs and cravings were not merely satisfied but extinguished — hence the complete satisfaction provided by such a simple and elemental structure.

The desires of Camp Nirvana's builders were similar, but not identical to, the motivations of the Rusticators who had first come to the Maine coast a few decades before. The Rusticators sought to recover an intimate understanding of nature — a relationship they saw as corrupted by modernity and urbanization — and to that end desired a built environment for themselves that reflected their regard for nature and mankind's true place in nature. But the built environment they chose or that was adapted to and evolved from their principles — namely Downing's designs and eventually the Shingle style — was nevertheless a distinctly man-made, initially pastoral, built environment, established on European models and expressive of man in close harmony with, but distinct from, nature. Camp Nirvana, in contrast, was a near-total return to nature, and barriers between the individual and the environment were as far as possible eliminated altogether. Architecture had provided a frame, or reference point, for the Rusticators, a built environment that provided comforts that were not extravagant but were amenities nonetheless, conceived in forms that reinforced the connection between man and nature. Camp Nirvana provided hearth and shelter only. No frame or perspective was needed to reinforce a concept of man in harmony with nature, for under that lean-to on Squam Lake, the smoke of the campfire filling the air and rain falling inches from their feet, Closson, Hough, and their contemporaries were not just in harmony with nature but fully immersed in it.

Camp Nirvana was not unique in its primitive and intimate approach to recreation. Camping and fishing expeditions had been a popular summer pastime for college students for several decades; Henry David Thoreau had made a similar camp, also shared with a college roommate, on Flint's Pond in Massachusetts, in 1837, eight years before his sojourn at Walden. In Maine, Student's Island at Mooselookmeguntic Lake is named for Yale University students who camped there in the 1840s. Nirvana is exceptional, though, in what followed it, both socially and architecturally. One of Camp Nirvana's visitors, Ernest Berkeley Balch, took Closson's and Hough's example as inspiration for a more organized form of camping, created for younger boys and dedicated to educational activities that were complementary to but quite distinct from academic studies pursued during the school year. In 1881 Balch opened Camp Chocorua (so named for the site's commanding view of that peak) on one of Squam's islands, with six campers and a single building. Camp life was centered on physical activity, sports, woods lore, and the development of useful outdoor skills, all presented with an eye toward moral development and self-reliance as preparation of campers for life in the larger, non-primitive, world. From this early experiment — Chocorua lasted only nine years, to 1890 — grew the American summer camp movement, first limited to boys but extended to girls by 1900.[3]

Among Camp Chocorua's alumni were the brothers Harold J. and Julian L.

Coolidge, who attended the camp in its last years. They conveyed their enthusiasm for camp life and for Squam to their parents, Joseph Randolph and Julia Gardiner Coolidge, in such vivid and convincing terms that the family bought property at the lake in 1893 – a farm near the lake's shore – which they maintained as a working farm and summer retreat. Coolidge family members continued to buy land for several generations, building camps both on the lake shore and on islands in the lake, creating an extended family compound.

The Coolidges, one of several extended families who kept a number of summer residences at Squam, adhered in their own building to the minimal architectural principles of Camp Nirvana and Camp Chocorua. By family tradition, young men of the family built their own camps, fashioned in a style more permanent and less primitive than Camp Nirvana, but not far from it in spirit and intent. The buildings were small, single-story structures with one or at most a few rooms, built near the shore but screened from it partially by forest, so that their presence was not obvious from the water; in fact, the lake was not always visible from the camp. These camps used architecture designed for the inhabitant, not for the external viewer; they were not intended to make a social statement or convey a visual message to an onlooker but to support – minimally – the activities and experience of the occupant. In their original form, many of the Coolidge camps were completely open on the side fac-

A Coolidge camp imagined at Squam Lake, nineteenth century. The front entrance and gable end above the entrance are completely open, establishing a connection between indoors and out not very distant from that at Camp Nirvana.

ing the water, with no partition, glass, or even screen dividing interior from exterior. In this way, the domestic realm of the hearth was again – as it was at Camp Nirvana – immersed in the surrounding realm of forest and lake. The camp, still essential in its capacity as shelter and distinct from its surroundings by virtue of its uniquely human purpose, is nonetheless *in* the landscape, rather than a frame or lens through which nature may be perceived to advantage.

SILVER LAKE

Twenty miles to the northeast of Squam, a gentle and low ridge rises to separate the valley of the Merrimack River on the west from the southeastward-trending valley of the Saco River. Crossing that divide, the first broad valley one encounters contains Ossipee Lake and the Ossipee River, a tributary of the Saco, and at the very head of that valley, looking north toward the Saco valley proper, lies Silver Lake. Like Squam, Silver Lake drew early summer vacationers to its combination of lake and mountain scenery, but the entire Saco valley region had had an even earlier attraction as a destination for the first nineteenth-century artists exploring the unfolding American landscape.

The concepts of the picturesque and the sublime were of special interest to American landscape painters, who, working initially from the late-eighteenth-century Gothic understanding of the sublime, entered the American wilderness not long after the earliest settlers.[4] There they found in abundance those wild and powerful elements of nature that characterized the Gothic sense of the sublime, including storms and natural disasters that were the evidence of divine power over mankind. The death of the Willey family in 1826, in a landslide outside their homestead in Crawford Notch, immediately southwest of Mount Washington, was the very embodiment of this understanding of the sublime, and the event as well as its physical setting drew the first wave of artists and writers to the White Mountains. Their creative works constituted the first "advertising" of the White Mountain region to the public (as many of the same group did some years later on the Maine coast), while the artists themselves were among the fledgling White Mountain tourist industry's first customers.

The Saco valley, winding among the lower mountains and hills south of Mount Washington, held a particular aesthetic attraction. This was a pastoral and picturesque haven in the large, wilder realm of the mountains, increasingly so as trees were cleared, soil cultivated, and the uninhabited country slowly domesticated and altered by the appearance of buildings drawn in equal measure from Colonial traditions and A. J. Downing's own vision of the picturesque. Beyond the peaceful valley, however, rose the still untamed White Mountains, scene of the Willey family's misfortune and unabatedly fierce in its climate and geography. The juxtaposition of the two visions, the sublime towering over the picturesque, symbolized not only the majesty of nature, but came also to represent the intrepidity of man's penetration of the wilderness, and the emerging American view of wilderness as representative of vast potential rather than as a threat. Even the understanding of sublimity was shifted by this new view, as American forests and mountains came to be depicted in landscape art as scenes of peace and harmony, inviting to the explorer and offering the promise of wealth and resource to a growing nation.[5] It was an ideal subject for a group of American landscape painters (the White Mountain School, several of whom would also become part of the Hudson River School) whose work presented new interpretations and attitudes toward nature, the relationship between man and nature, and the aesthetic meaning of wilderness.

The prominence given by landscape artists to the White Mountains and their immediate surroundings drew travelers from across the northeast. Many came seeking not just to satisfy their curiosity about these places but also to experience the pastoral landscape themselves for extended periods as guests at a growing number of hotels as well as at private houses, either converted from farms or built specially as summer homes. Access to the Saco valley region from the south was originally by wagon up the Saco River from the coast – a full day's journey from Portland to Conway – but in the 1870s the Portsmouth, Great Falls & Conway Railroad extended a line north along the eastern border of New Hampshire, connecting points to the south with Union, Wakefield, Ossipee, Madison (where the railroad ran along the shore of Silver Lake), and eventually Conway and North Conway. This railroad improved the access to lakes and hills on the southeast side of the White Mountains particularly from the Boston area, and Bostonians, including many academics, came to represent a prominent fraction of the region's summer residents.

WINTER ROAD HILL – W. D. HOWE HOUSE

By the last decades of the nineteenth century, the area including Conway, Madison, Chocorua, Silver Lake, and other nearby communities had become a remarkably intellectually oriented summer colony. Summer residents included the brothers philosopher William James and novelist Henry James, Harvard mathematician William Osgood, Boston minister and peace advocate Edward Cummings, and later his son, the poet E. E. Cummings. Edward Cummings was an acquaintance of William James, and may have been introduced to the region by James, who owned a house in the nearby town of Chocorua.

In 1899, Cummings bought a farm a short distance north of Silver Lake and made it into a family retreat. Cummings's farm, called Joy Farm after its previous owner, farmer Ephraim Joy, came to comprise more than 300 acres. In 1905, Cummings and his wife, Rebecca, bought another large piece of land along the eastern shore of Silver Lake, on which they built two more houses, both designed by Cummings.

ABOVE: *Winter Road Hill, Silver Lake, New Hampshire (E. Cummings, ca 1913), view from north. Winter Road Hill was designed according to vernacular examples seen in Norway by the original builder, Edward Cummings. The traditional features he used include the broad eaves and overhanging upper story to shelter the walls beneath from water and snow, and the broad, shallow-pitched roof, intended to hold a heavy insulating winter snow cover. The opening in the roof is original, but not a Norwegian vernacular feature.*

LEFT: *A typical Norwegian rural vernacular timber design, similar to what Cummings might have seen in Norway in 1910.*

Winter Road Hill, Silver Lake, New Hampshire (E. Cummings, ca. 1913), main room with side-by-side corner hearths. These are another traditional Norwegian design; the masonry walls behind the hearth reflect heat from the fire back into the room, and smoke is trapped in the enclosing canopy above. The heavy timbers are typical of climates where significant snow loads must be supported in winter. The rather low roof pitch is also a typical northern design — one of two roof designs specific to snowy climates, actually. In regions where winters are cold and snow loads are substantial but not overwhelming — interior regions of Scandinavia and Alaska, for example — roofs were traditionally built with a low pitch to hold a thick snow cover and insulate the roof. In extremely wet climates, however, such as coastal mountains in northern Norway, snow loads can overwhelm even heavily built roofs, and the traditional design here is the very steeply pitched A-frame.

Cummings, a professor of sociology and political science at Harvard, and later a minister ordained in the Congregational Church, traveled widely as part of his association with the Boston-based World Peace Foundation, for which he served as general secretary. Cummings had developed an enthusiasm for Norwegian vernacular architecture while in Norway in 1910, and the second of the two lakeshore houses, Winter Road Hill, built in 1912 or 1913, is based on rural Norwegian designs.

Winter Road Hill was sold in 1930 to Cummings's friend and relative by marriage Will D. Howe following Cummings's death in 1930. The house, known as Winter Road Hill, then remained in the Howe family for more than seventy years.[6] Howe, an influential figure in American literature, was as much a part of Silver Lake's intellectual circle as the members of the Cummings family. Initially a professor of English literature, Howe moved between the academic and commercial publishing worlds, becoming an editor at Harcourt, Brace and Howe, later a founding member of Scribner's, and ultimately returning to academia at Emory University and the University of Georgia, where he died in 1946. Silver Lake and Winter Road Hill remained the family's summer retreat throughout these years.

The house is composed of a single square mass, sheltered under a broad, low-pitched roof with substantial overhangs. The extensive exterior ornamentation typical of many Scandinavian houses is absent here, replaced by continuous cedar shingling,

Winter Road Hill, Silver Lake, New Hampshire (E. Cummings, ca. 1913).

ABOVE: *Master bedroom. The heavily timbered roof, wide pine paneling, and corner fireplace all reflect Cummings's desire to capture the details of the house's Norwegian progenitors.*

LEFT: *Second-floor hall and study. Bedrooms and a third-floor interior balcony all open onto this second-floor space, much more an additional room than a corridor. Cummings's study was here, his desk placed by the windows in the background.*

but tall posts supporting the overhanging roof and portions of the second story reflect the building's heavy timber origins.

The interior of Winter Road Hill is a remarkable departure from Craftsman and other contemporary architectural influences so visible in many other New England summer cottages. Cummings's design captured certain characteristics of Scandinavian design succinctly, including open floor plans and spaces designed for multiple uses, similar in concept to the Shingle style's open floor plan, but very different in appearance and feeling. A double fireplace, with hearths placed side-by-side in mirrored inglenooks, dominates the main room. The inscription over the hearths was added in the 1930s after the house was owned by the Howe family. It reads, "And well I saw the firelight like a flight of homely elves," a line from *A Christmas at Sea*, by Robert Louis Stevenson, whose poetry Howe had written about in his Ph.D. dissertation.

Fireplaces of the same design appear on the second floor, in the master bedroom and in an open hall surrounding the main staircase. The open plan of the ground floor is extended upward through this staircase to the second floor, and beyond, visually, to a third floor balcony that looks back down into the second floor hall (where Howe had his study) and the main stairs leading back to the main ground-floor room. Bedrooms open off the second floor hall, each with its own sleeping porch. The porches, open to the outdoors except for screens but still sheltered under the large roof eaves, form a link, essential to so many summer houses, between indoors and outdoors. Within the house, the juxtaposition of the open and interconnected spaces with heavy, enclosing framing gives the house an ordered, protective, and sheltered feeling (surely a key design element in Scandinavian buildings set in cold boreal environments), but not a sense of isolation either from other occupants of the house or the environment.

WILLIAM F. OSGOOD COTTAGE

W. F. Osgood Cottage, Silver Lake, New Hampshire (L. Knapp, architect, 1916), dish closet. A simple but highly effective detail that the occupants of the house treasure. Dishes are served and passed back for washing through a counter pass-through to the left but stored after washing and removed for meals through this cupboard.

In 1916, a short distance from Winter Road Hill along the shore of Silver Lake, the Harvard mathematician William F. Osgood (1864–1943) built his own summer cottage, designed by architect Lucia Knapp, the daughter of Fredrick Knapp, a close friend of Osgood's. Osgood was born and raised in Boston and educated in mathematics at Harvard and in Germany. Returning to the United States in 1890, Osgood became a professor of mathematics at Harvard, where he remained until 1933. Osgood's introduction to Silver Lake may have been through Fredrick Knapp, a school headmaster from Duxbury, Massachusetts, and land owner at the lake, although by the first decade of the twentieth century a number of Harvard faculty had summer homes in the area, and Osgood's knowledge of the place would easily have come from one of them. In any case, it was Knapp who sold Osgood the land on which his cottage sits. Knapp himself had already built a house on Silver Lake a

few years earlier (this burned in the late 1960s), also designed by Knapp's daughter Lucia, and sharing various design elements seen in the Osgood house.

The Osgood cottage is a simply massed building with in-cut screen porches but otherwise composed of a single gable-ended unit. Lucia Knapp's design (drawn up on fourteen sheets of vellum) is unusually detailed for a cottage and gives extensive engineering details for construction, not only for framing but for masonry, the house's water system, and details for windows that open by sliding sideways along tracks.

Knapp's design is very compact (the house occupies a twenty-eight by thirty-two-foot perimeter) and includes a number of space-saving features, including, typically, a compact staircase and upstairs corridor of irregular dimension to accommodate access to several bedrooms, and less typically, the sliding windows and a built-in dish cabinet accessible from both the kitchen and the dining room. Since Knapp was a friend of Osgood's, it is reasonable to suppose that Osgood communicated with her on details of the design and may have contributed significantly to those details. The house remains very nearly unchanged today from its original design, and with seven bedrooms and a sleeping porch, it is well suited for summertime occupation by a family of several generations.

W. F. Osgood Cottage, Silver Lake, New Hampshire (L. Knapp, architect, 1916), exterior overview. Architect Lucia Knapp envisioned an orderly but informal cottage, surrounded by tall pines and looking out over Silver Lake. She placed the iconic profile of Mt. Chocorua in the background.

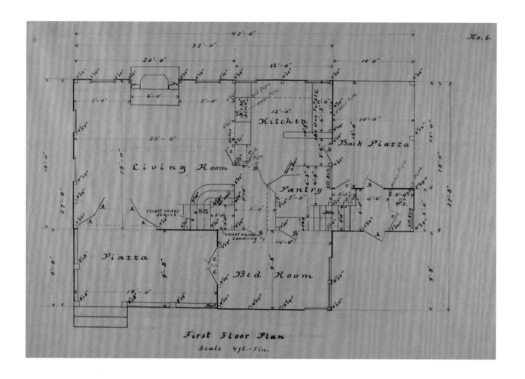

First Floor Plan

Scale 4ft.=1in.

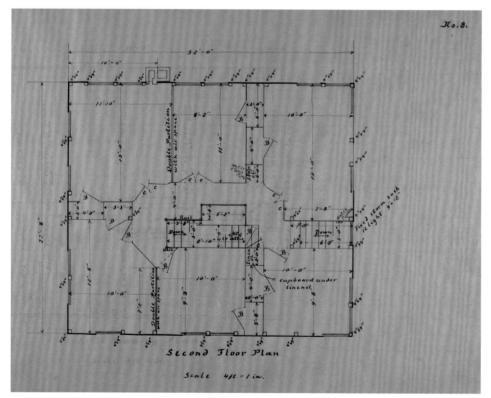

Second Floor Plan

Scale 4ft.=1in.

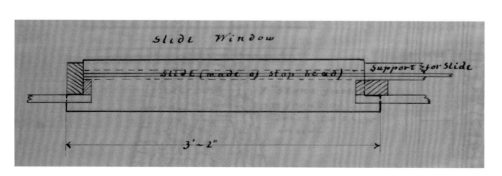

Slide Window

W. F. Osgood Cottage, Silver Lake, New Hampshire (L. Knapp, architect, 1916).

LEFT: *Ground floor plan. This is a very detailed plan for a house of this type. Details that were often the invention of the builder, like the pass-through dish cupboard, in this case are shown on the drawing.*

MIDDLE: *Second floor plan. Again, a high level of detail for a summer cottage. Note the specification of interior walls with "double partition with air space"; this was an effort to provide some level of soundproofing between rooms that were not separated by closets.*

BOTTOM: *Detail for sliding window.*

W. F. Osgood Cottage, Silver Lake, New Hampshire (L. Knapp, architect, 1916).

ABOVE: *Second-floor hall. Here is another example of the efficient use of corridor space on the second floor. Compare this photograph to the second-floor drawing to see how the use of double doors opening onto the bedrooms works to reduce cramping of the interior space and a sense of isolation of individual interior spaces.*

LEFT: *Main staircase. Without the curved steps at the bottom, a banister would be required below the fourth-step landing, and the staircase would have been cramped and cut off from the rest of the ground floor.*

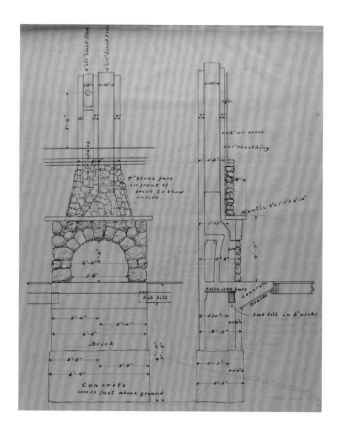

RANDOLPH

W. F. Osgood Cottage, Silver Lake, New Hampshire (L. Knapp, architect, 1916).

ABOVE LEFT: *Plan showing fireplace detail.*

ABOVE RIGHT: *The builder followed the drawn specifications provided for the fireplace precisely.*

Passing the height of land at Pinkham Notch, I looked up to the west into the dark bowls of Tuckerman's and Huntington's ravines, then passed the base of the Mt. Washington Auto Road, gated for the night. Further on, the Osgood Ridge on Mt. Madison sloped down into the valley bottom ahead of me, holding the northern side of the Great Gulf Wilderness in its embrace. The rocks on Madison's summit stood out faintly in silhouette against the pale blue night sky.

Turning off Route 16 onto the Dolly Copp road to take the shortcut around the east end of Mt. Madison to Randolph, I entered the dark and close forest at the base of the Osgood Ridge. Tall maple and beech trees met overhead, and in the light of my headlights the dirt road wound ahead of me like a narrow path. Near here lived Dolly and Hayes Copp, homesteaders from the 1830s to the 1880s on Daniel Pinkham's road from Jackson to Randolph. Pinkham had envisioned a great road through the Notch, carrying travelers to explore the mountains and farmers and loggers to tame the landscape. Travelers came, but the Notch was cold and its soil stony. Farmers approached the White Mountains cautiously, picking the good bottom land in the valleys as far up as the towns of Bartlett and Intervale to the south, or Shelburne to the north; only Hayes and Dolly came into the heart of the mountains, right at the feet of Mt. Madison, with the slopes of Osgood Ridge running down to their doorstep. It was not an auspicious place to pick out a living from among the rocks, and by the start of the twentieth century, the Copp home was abandoned, Hayes and Dolly had parted ways, and the forest was closing in on their home-

stead, the trees springing up and joining over their clearing, as they closed now over my head in the darkness as the road cut north through the forest toward Randolph.

With no town square or cluster of businesses, Randolph is sparsely distributed along four miles of rock-strewn valley and hillside in Coos County, dominated by mountains. Adams and Madison, the northernmost summits of the Presidential Range, stand immediately above the town on the south side of the Moose River valley. The town lies in the narrow valley bottom and on the valley's north side, facing the summits four thousand feet above and only three miles distant. Randolph is high and cold, situated on the divide separating the drainages of the Connecticut and Androscoggin Rivers, and thus as far from the early routes of access as one can get in this part of the state. The town was settled late: Randolph's first settlers appeared in the 1790s, thirty years after the end of the French and Indian War. Originally

Lewis Cottage with mounts Madison and Adams in the background, Randolph New Hampshire.

granted in 1772 to John Durand of London, Randolph was named in 1824 by New Hampshire Governor Levi Woodbury when the town was formally incorporated. Monuments in the Randolph cemetery mark the graves of the early settlers, including a handful of Revolutionary War soldiers, and family names and dates chronicle the modest growth of the town through the nineteenth and twentieth centuries. Farming, logging, and later tourism were the principal occupations, although the farming must have been as tough here as anywhere in northern New England. Today the year-round population is somewhat less than four hundred, about the same as it was in the 1880s. Land cleared for pasture generations ago has grown back to forest, and the stone walls that bordered the pastures of the nineteenth century are now low, moss-covered lines, nearly invisible, straight paths marking the disappearance of an old way of life into the dense woods.

Randolph natives were quick to take advantage of the growing popularity of the White Mountains as a tourist destination following the end of the Civil War. Some summer lodgers were taken at private houses in the 1850s, but the rise of Randolph as a summer destination occurred principally in the late 1870s and early 1880s with the establishment of three small hotels: the Ravine House, the Kelsey Cottage (later known as the Mountain View House), and the Mount Crescent House. All were small summer-only establishments (although the Ravine House operated in winter in the early decades of the twentieth century), accessed by wagon from Gorham and by railroad through the Randolph Valley after 1892. Hiking, social events set in woods and mountains, and trailbuilding in the earliest days were the threads that made the fabric of Randolph's summer community. The writings of Thomas Starr King in the 1850s had drawn adventurous visitors to the northern peaks and to Randolph in particular. When the Ravine House was opened by local farmer (and later mountain guide) Laban Watson in 1877, a group of energetic Appalachian Mountain Club trailbuilders already familiar with this side of the mountains took up summer residence. During the 1880s Ravine House guests, working with local innkeepers and guides, built some fifty miles of trails in Randolph and on the north slopes of Adams and Madison. Summer activities thus included much manual labor as rocks were moved, trees cleared, and paths graded in building the first trails. These trails were among the earliest parts of the extensive trail system that now covers the Presidential Range. The leading early trailbuilders – locals and summer visitors alike – were distinctive characters, many of whom are now remembered in White Mountain place and trail names like Edmand's Col, the Cook Path, Lowe's Path, and Watson Path. Around these leaders gathered other summer visitors, first at the Ravine House, later at the Kelsey Cottage and Mt. Crescent House, and ultimately in cottages. From these the nucleus of the Randolph summer community was formed. The labors were punctuated by group activities – picnics, group hikes, amateur theatricals – mostly taking place in the mountains or closely associated with them.

In the early days, before the construction of summer cottages, the hotels provided lodging, meals, guides for the mountains, and transportation to and from the railroad. By the closing years of the nineteenth century, despite the convenience and comforts of hotel life, many of the summer visitors sought their own dwellings after a few seasons of hotel life.

Long-term economic considerations or increased comfort and privacy may have been motivations for people who intended to become summer visitors for the long term, but letters and published descriptions from that time suggest that a sense of personal investment and belonging to the community was a factor in their decisions as well. Local craftsmen and landowners responded to this demand, and starting as

Ravine House daybook entry for July 24, 1883.

early as 1896, some existing buildings were converted to use for a few hardy summer visitors. In the next thirty-five years, new construction and subdivision of formerly agricultural land boomed, and dozens of summer houses of a wide range of size and styles were built, first in Randolph valley and later on the hill to the north. The summer residents living in their own houses quickly outnumbered those staying in the hotels. Until the 1960s, the hotels continued to provide meals and other services to summer residents and remained the focal point of summer social life in Randolph.[7]

JOHN H. BOOTHMAN

John H. Boothman (1868–1952).

Among the town residents responsible for Randolph's twentieth-century growth as a tourist destination was the Randolph builder and Mt. Crescent House owner John H. Boothman (1868–1952). The Boothman family operated the Mt. Crescent House from 1923 to 1971, and from around 1902 to 1950 Boothman built some eighty-five houses all over Randolph. He acted both as builder and real estate agent, buying, selling, and trading land in the town throughout his career. His papers were saved by his descendants, including construction ledgers, plans, deed transactions, day books, and other materials that detail his life and activities in extraordinary breadth and depth.

Aspects of John Boothman's career can be seen in detail in those records. He was evidently a meticulous, pragmatic individual who maintained many lines of work; as well as his work as a hotel keeper, land agent, and builder, Boothman was also a community leader who served as a state representative and town selectman. His notes and correspondence suggest a person perfectly capable of keeping his many lines of activity going simultaneously, with the assistance and participation of his wife, Edith (daughter of Ravine House proprietor Laban Watson), who probably did much of the actual account and record keeping. Boothman's commitment to the advancement of the town of Randolph as a tourist destination is evident not only in his building but also in his civic leadership in the community. It was Boothman who, in 1910, proposed that the town form an association to restore the network of hiking trails, at that time nearly obliterated by logging. That association became the Randolph Mountain Club, which continues today to maintain trails and huts in the northern Presidential Range. Boothman explored the mountains himself in both summer and winter and supported an early (but unrealized) effort to bring skiing to Randolph, as can be seen in a letter to a summer client from the winter of 1939:

> *The winter business in this section also lookes very good most of it centered in the South side from Conway to Pinkham Notch. Jack and Mr. Pote was invited to the Eastern Slope Inn New years evening to see moving pictures in colors, "Skii America First." The Inn was crowded with a capasity of 275 people, The smaller places were also reported full. Nothing definite has been done about a skii trail in Randolph, but we are still*

working on the proposition with the idea to induce the U.S. Forest service to build a
trail from Ravine House to Mt Adams.[8]

Boothman was educated in Randolph and nearby Gorham,[9] and there is no
record of his ever traveling far from Randolph (his farthest travels may not have been
beyond the state capital at Concord). Again, typical for his time and place, there is no
evidence of his having any formal training in architecture or design. Like the vast
majority of builders of his time, he learned the building trades locally. As a young
man Boothman worked for a contractor named William Lyman McGivney in the
nearby mill town of Berlin until about 1898, when he established himself as an independent contractor in Randolph.[10] A few houses probably built by McGivney, but
extensively altered, stand today in Berlin.[11] They show little similarity to Boothman's
Randolph houses, and offer few clues as to Boothman's early stylistic influences. Ber-

House built by William Lyman
McGiveney, Boothman's mentor.
Berlin, New Hampshire (detail).

lin was founded in 1829, later than towns south of the White Mountains or closer to
the Connecticut River, and its infrastructure was built up principally during the first
decades of the twentieth century, coincident with its fastest population growth.
Accordingly, widespread New England styles of the late eighteenth and early nineteenth century, such as Federal or Greek Revival, have almost no representation here.
The dominant early house type in Berlin, and the style with which Boothman probably had the most experience while working for McGivney, was the nationally widespread four-square house. Queen Anne and early twentieth-century Shingle-style
derivatives are also fairly common in Berlin, and their presence there supports the
likelihood that Boothman was exposed to the style and well aware of its potential.

ABOVE LEFT: *Robert A. Andrews house (Fay Fount, 1903), view from west by E. W. Blood. A classic example of Shingle style on a moderate scale. This and The Thornbush may be John H. Boothman's earliest Randolph houses.*

ABOVE RIGHT: *Augustus Simonds house (The Thornbush, 1902), view from east. Guy Shorey photo. Shingle elements (uninterrupted shingle cladding, deep gambrel roof, and a trim board closing the gable end suggestive of a pent roof) applied to Colonial Revival plan and massing match this house more compatibly with its forest surroundings.*

Boothman's first known works as an independent contractor in Randolph include three houses built between 1900 and 1903, all of them placed very near one another on the town's main road running east–west through the Moose River valley. While built originally for summer residents, the houses were constructed for year-round occupancy and were used as such for many years by later owners; all are large with interiors finished in conventional styles (plaster or center bead interior paneling). These three houses may not have been Boothman's own designs. One, built for Robert A. Andrews of Cambridge, Massachusetts (and named Fay-Fount during a later period when it was part of the property of the Ravine House hotel), is a Shingle-style building, ornate by Randolph standards at that time. It is unlike Boothman's other work in Randolph but very close to conventional Shingle-style examples built in Berlin. The other two houses of this group, Wollaston Lodge (built for Clarence Reid of Stamford, Connecticut, 1900) and The Thornbush (built for Augustus Simonds of Haverhill, Massachusetts, 1902) are an amalgam of Shingle-style exterior elements and Colonial Revival symmetry and massing. Eclectic combinations of various elements of other established styles were fairly common in northern New England during this period; houses with forms derived from Colonial Revival or Four-Square styles, covered in uninterrupted shingle cladding (as well as other characteristic Shingle-style elements), are fairly common in New England towns that experienced significant growth in housing stock at the close of the 1800s and opening decade of the twentieth century.[12]

These three houses also suggest Boothman's early awareness of the contextual differences between Berlin and Randolph. At the turn of the twentieth century, Berlin was a small city experiencing rapid growth, industrialization, and modernization,[13] while Randolph was developing (if not growing in size) as a summer destination with rural character and a natural mountain setting as its chief assets. Fay-Fount, while a very attractive example of the formal Shingle style, is nonetheless an anomaly in Randolph; the simpler forms and more rustic finish of Wollaston Lodge and The Thornbush are more consistent with Randolph's mountainous and rural nature. It is likely that Boothman, and his clients, as well, perceived this difference, for virtually no houses in the urbane style of Fay-Fount appeared again in Randolph, while shingle cladding became nearly ubiquitous.

DUDLEY HOUSE

A fourth house, built in 1902 on Randolph Hill, was Boothman's earliest summer-only cottage, built for Albertus and Francis Dudley. Family records indicate that Boothman built the house, but nothing is known of the details of the construction. Boothman's records are not available for 1902, although a later ledger details a smaller construction project (possibly a house addition) for the Dudleys in July 1914. The interior of the cottage was paneled many years after its original construction so any framing and finish elements typical of Boothman's practices are hidden. The house is a fine example of interpenetrating interior and exterior space, the ground-level porch slicing into its east end, opening a view literally through the house to the mountains when viewed from the north side, the main approach to the house. Porches were used to the same purpose in Fay-Fount, but the effect is more

Albertus Dudley house, Randolph, New Hampshire (J. H. Boothman, 1903), view from north.

dramatic in the Dudley cottage, owing to the house's much smaller scale, and the correspondingly larger influence of the void created by the undercut porch.

Another distinctive feature of the Dudley house, one characteristic of Boothman's smaller cottages, and especially those near one of the town's hotels, is its extraordinarily small kitchen. While some Randolph summer houses included separate space evidently intended for servant's quarters, and had kitchen layouts isolated from dining and living spaces, the smaller cottages were clearly made for occupancy by a family unit, with all space, including the kitchen, shared equally. No facilities were provided for elaborate cooking and entertaining, perhaps in large part because the hotels provided the meals and setting for larger social functions. Many of the Randolph Hill summer residents took most of their daily meals at the Mountain View House or the Mt. Crescent House,[14] using their own cottage kitchens only for simple preparation of breakfast or lunch.

Albertus Dudley house, Randolph, New Hampshire (J. H. Boothman, 1903), kitchen.

JUDSON HOUSE

In 1903, Dr. Charles Judson of Philadelphia contracted with John Boothman for a large house for summer use, to be built in the Randolph valley facing the summits of the northern Presidential Range. This is the earliest extant Boothman design for which both his drawings and ledger records are available. The drawings for the house show, typically, simple elevations and floor plans only. No detailed instructions on trim or finish are given, although this might not be expected in this case, where Boothman made the drawings for his own use and thus did not require explicit details. The main room bears an unmistakable resemblance to an illustration of an English building, named Falkewood, which appeared in a 1906 English publication, *Houses and Gardens: Arts and Crafts Interiors.*[15] The figure actually appeared after the construction of the Judson house, and there is no indication that Boothman

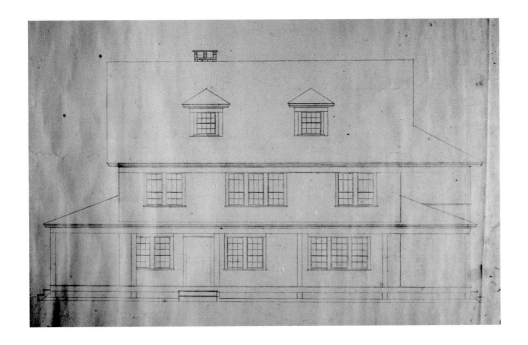

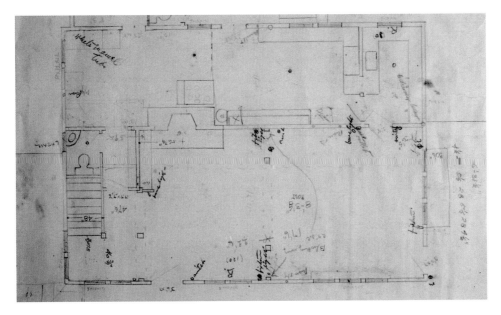

TOP: *J. H. Boothman drawing for Judson house (1904), south elevation. Collection of J. H. Boothman.*

LEFT: *J. H. Boothman drawing for Judson house (1904), ground floor plan with annotations. Collection of J. H. Boothman.*

Judson house, Randolph, New Hampshire (J. H. Boothman, 1904). Exterior view from southeast. Note the differences in rooflines between the house as built and the drawings; the gable ends shown on the drawings are replaced by hips in the actual construction. Changes at this level could easily have been accomplished without changes in the drawings. Detailed framing calculations (such as might have been used for mitre cuts in a hipped roof) were either not saved or possibly never needed.

knew of the Falkewood example, but some prior publication of this rendering may have been the starting point for Boothman's design, found either by Boothman himself or given to him by Dr. Judson.

Construction on the Judson house began in October 1903 with improvements to an access road and preparation of the foundation. Framing and enclosure proceeded through the winter, and by the spring of 1904, work started on plumbing, plaster and lathe, and interior finish carpentry. Boothman did not list his employees by name, but from the records of charges for labor, it appears that Boothman used a small crew of men of various levels of skill, ranging from laborers for digging the foundation to skilled craftsmen for framing, plaster work, masonry, and finish carpentry. Boothman himself was a skilled framing and finish carpenter, but, at least in his later work, he acted chiefly as a supervisor and as marker in a three-man mark/cut/nail crew like that used by Robie Norwood in Southwest Harbor.[16]

Finish work and furnishing continued through the summer of 1904, and after an inactive winter, the house was ready for occupancy by the summer of 1905. Boothman often furnished the houses he built; the Judson house is furnished with Boothman's own built-in and free-standing furniture as well as purchased furniture. Boothman's ledger shows the finishing touches being completed in May 1905 ("Drawer pulls $0.25" on May 25; "Paint for front door $0.50" on June 5); on June 28 the water was turned on, and the house presumably was occupied at this point. The ledger accounts show labor principally for maintenance and opening and closing of the house after this date. In 1903, at age thirty-five, Boothman charged three dollars per day for his own labor; the total cost for the Judson house was $4,660.[17]

The main room of the Judson house shows a very strong Arts-and-Crafts character, presumably the influence of the Falkewood rendering (or an equivalent), but

TOP: *Judson house, Randolph, New Hampshire (J. H. Boothman, 1904). Entry and staircase. The similarity to the 1906 Falkewood interior is obvious, although the drawing appeared two years after the Judson house was completed. Since Boothman drew the original plans for this house, it is possible that Judson knew of the Falkewood plan from some other source and gave it to Boothman as a stylistic model.*

ABOVE: *Falkewood interior. From* Houses and Gardens — Arts and Crafts Interiors, *by M. H. Baillie-Scott, originally published by George Newness, Ltd, 1906.*

Judson house, Randolph, New Hampshire (J. H. Boothman, 1904).

ABOVE LEFT: *Dining room with built-in bench and Craftsman-style table and chairs.*

ABOVE RIGHT: *Stairwell with Arts-and-Crafts-style pendant light fixture.*

the rest of the house is less "picturesque" (in the sense employed by Downing) and more symmetrical than classic examples of early Arts-and-Crafts and Craftsman designs. The house's exterior massing is a single rectangular block with a fairly high-hipped roof bearing two forward-facing gable dormers surrounded by a substantial porch. The exterior layout of the main façade is slightly asymmetrical but resembles a traditional three-bay side-gable common to a wide range of American styles. The contrast between the strong Arts-and-Crafts flavor of the main room and the well-proportioned but generally American vernacular style of the remainder of the house suggests that Boothman was expanding his awareness of design, employing new stylistic concepts (Arts-and-Crafts) in combination with traditional elements (more-or-less symmetrical side-gable massing) that he adjusted (through the use of unstained shingles instead of clapboards) to the more rural and natural character of the location.

BRICKELMEYER COTTAGE

Boothman built the Brickelmeyer cottage in 1914,[18] evidently using a plan in his possession obtained from The Craftsman Architects, a part of Gustav Stickley's Crafts-man enterprises that sold working drawings of houses featured in Stickley's magazine *The Craftsman*. Boothman followed the published floor plans and elevations closely but finished the interior – whose details were unspecified in the drawings in Booth-man's collection – simply, with stud frames sheathed on one side only in horizontally laid tongue-and-groove pine. This style was widely employed elsewhere in camp

Brickelmeyer Cottage, Randolph, New Hampshire.

RIGHT: *Craftsman Architects drawing for bungalow, front view. Collection of J. H. Boothman.*

BELOW RIGHT: *Craftsman Architects drawing for bungalow, side view. Collection of J. H. Boothman.*

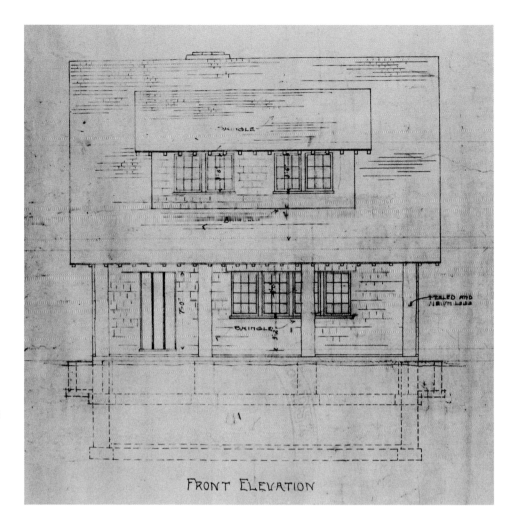

FRONT ELEVATION

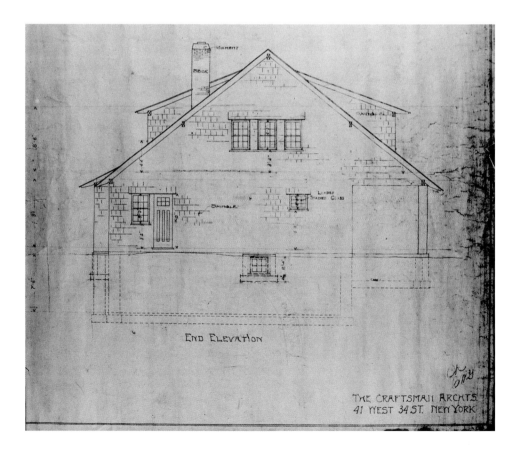

END ELEVATION

THE CRAFTSMAN ARCHTS.
41 WEST 34 ST. NEW YORK

Brickelmeyer Cottage, Randolph, New Hampshire (J. H. Booth-man, 1914), view from south. The house follows the Craftsman Architects plan almost exactly.

Brickelmeyer Cottage, Randolph, New Hampshire (J. H. Boothman, 1914).

RIGHT: *Second-floor bedroom. In summer cottages, second-floor rooms were often finished much more simply than ground-floor rooms. Here Booth-man retained his use of larger ceiling joists, however, and sheathed the walls in planed tongue-and-groove pine of similar quality to the ground-floor rooms.*

BELOW RIGHT: *Main room. Typi-cally for plans of this type and period, the structural details of the house were not specified in the Craftsman Archi-tects drawings. The use of larger and more widely spaced joists in the ceiling was Boothman's decision and antici-pates the exposed interior frames of many of his later houses.*

and cottage construction, but Boothman's implementation of it was unusual in his careful choice and arrangement of framing members. Rather than leave a conventionally framed stud wall unsheathed (for example as Robie Norwood did in Half Acre), Boothman chose larger, more widely spaced framing members to create a more open and uniform appearance. While Stickley and his Craftsman Architects company dealt extensively in interior design, the details of specific house interiors were typically described in general terms through illustrations rather than explicit inclusion in the working drawings.[19] The plans also left the calculations of loads and details of framing to the builder.[20] Boothman's framing here anticipates many of his later cottages, where he applied similar ideas in projects ranging from very simple houses of his own design to execution of architect's plans in more elaborate buildings.

WILL H. BRADLEY HOUSE

While John Boothman was establishing himself as a contractor specializing in summer cottages, some Randolph summer residents were building their own cottages or modifying existing buildings for summer use. George N. Cross, the author of the 1929 history *Randolph Old and New*, was possibly the first summer resident to establish himself and his family in a private house, a building erected in 1826 and variously used as a storage building and part of a starch factory. Cross bought the building in the fall of 1896 and converted it to a summer house over the course of the next three years.

A few years after George Cross built his cottage, the designer and illustrator Will H. Bradley arrived in Randolph with his family. Bradley, born in 1868, was a native of Boston but had spent most of his adult life in the Midwest. There he had established a national reputation as an artist, illustrator, designer, and typographer in the

Will H. Bradley House, Randolph, New Hampshire.

BELOW LEFT: *Exterior view, illustration from "Exterior of the Bradley house, closing the series."* Will Bradley, Ladies' Home Journal *19(11), August 1902.*

BELOW RIGHT: *Front (north) façade. Bradley's Arts-and-Crafts influences are evident in the shape and variety of casement and fixed windows. The gambrel roof and cross-gable echo Bradley's suggested exterior in his* Ladies' Home Journal *article of 1902.*

STILL ANOTHER SUGGESTION

Will H. Bradley House, Randolph, New Hampshire .

ABOVE LEFT: *Interior view and details, "A Bradley house: the dining-room." Will Bradley, Ladies' Home Journal 19(11) January 1902.*

ABOVE RIGHT: *Inglenook and fireplace. The inglenook, or sheltered enclosure for a fireplace, is a focal point in Arts-and-Crafts and Craftsman styles. A revival of medieval fireplaces, which before the development of efficient chimney designs required a roofed enclosure to contain smoke, the inglenook's space here is defined by flanking benches that distinguish it from the rest of the room without isolating it. A short partition is visible on the left, a ubiquitous feature of Arts-and-Crafts designs that breaks up a large central room visually and identifies different spaces without isolating them.*

Chicago area, most notably through his involvement with the trade journal *The Inland Printer*. Bradley returned to the East Coast in 1894, opening his own studio in Springfield, Massachusetts. He later relocated to New York City and Millburn, New Jersey, and eventually retired to live in California with his daughter until his death in 1957. Bradley's design work was closely associated with the Art Nouveau and Arts-and-Crafts movements, principally in graphic design, but also in architecture. In a series of articles published in the *Ladies' Home Journal* between 1902 and 1905, Bradley described features of "A Bradley House," wherein he applied his design ideas to domestic architecture, including designs to be built on a decidedly modest scale (one installment of the series is entitled, "Two Ideas for a $1000 House").[21]

Bradley's articles were part of a much larger series published in the *Ladies' Home Journal* between 1895 and 1915, during the tenure of editor Edward Bok. Through the venue of the *Journal*, Bok energetically promoted domestic architecture designed according to principles of the Progressive movement, including aesthetics, health, new technology, and efficiency.[22] Bradley's Arts-and-Crafts sensibilities and his aesthetic affinity with Progressive designers like Gustav Stickley made his house designs especially suitable for Bok's ambitions.

Bradley and his family appear in the Mt. Crescent House guest register on July 1, 1903, but other written records suggest that he may have been in Randolph as early as 1900. Whatever his earlier appearances, Bradley was engaged in building his own house in Randolph in 1906. The design of the house may be safely assumed to be his own, given his writings on architecture, and there is no evidence that John Booth-man was involved in the house's construction. Indeed, Bradley later built a new house for himself in Millburn, New Jersey, in 1915, and is known to have done a large portion of the work there himself.[23] He did at least have assistance in Randolph, for one contemporary diary record from Randolph resident Eldena Hunt records that "Mr. Bradley's carpenter, Mr. Kilgore was here . . . trying to get boarded."[24] As a contractor and energetic developer of real estate in Randolph, Boothman would clearly have been well aware of the construction of the Bradley house. It is likely that Bradley's simple but sophisticated designs and interiors influenced Boothman's own work, for many similarities can be found between the Bradley house and Boothman's later work in features like interior finish and built-in furniture – the very details typically left out of published architectural plans of the day. But Bradley's specific influence on Boothman can only be guessed at, for Boothman's houses evolved simultaneously in sophistication and simplicity from this time to the end of his career – probably a product of his own creative impulses combined with his exposure to the broad variety of taste, style, and culture typical of Randolph's eclectic summer population.

Boothman continued to build houses, either of his own design, using guidance from books and illustrations, or from full architectural plans. His work was almost entirely composed of houses for summer residents, although he did work on several huts on Mts. Madison and Adams, including rebuilding the Appalachian Mountain Club's Madison Spring Hut in 1916. His personal style, marked by patterns of interior framing, a combination of exposed framing and finished interior detail, absence of purely decorative ornament, unstained and unfinished wood surfaces, and layout and massing strongly influenced by Craftsman designs, is evident in all his houses. But even with the benefit of the extensive records preserved by the Boothman family, it is difficult to determine exactly how that style evolved, particularly without cer-

Will H. Bradley House, Randolph, New Hampshire (1906).

BELOW LEFT: *View from west*

BELOW RIGHT: *Window alcove. These simple casement windows appear in a variety of shapes and sizes throughout the house, and are built of simple one-inch pine muntins dividing casement wings into panes of different sizes. Bradley's use of these divided windows illustrates the critical role of windows in the visual balance between indoors and outdoors: the window is a frame through which the outside world is viewed. The viewer is neither entirely in the landscape (as was very nearly the case, for example, at Camp Nirvana) nor entirely isolated from it, and the muntins, unobtrusively blocking part of the view, reinforce that relationship.*

Will H. Bradley House, Randolph, New Hampshire (1906), ingle-nook window, exterior view.

tain knowledge of which houses were entirely his own design. Still, on the evidence of his first four Randolph houses (1900–1903), Boothman was a mature builder with full command of conventional styles from the very outset of his Randolph building career, so his style developed as an adaptation to a new clientele as opposed to emerging expertise. Furthermore, his personal style is expressed to varying degrees in nearly every one of his houses; in only a few cases (and these occur later in his career) did he build a house entirely to an architect's specification down to interior details.

BARTLETT COTTAGE

In 1919, Boothman completed a small and very simple cottage for the "Misses Bartlett." This house, entirely of Boothman's design, was built for $3,000 (materials and labor), and some details suggest it was designed around strict budgetary limits. The house is among the smallest and simplest of Boothman's projects, composed of a single gable-end unit containing one in-cut porch – a very simple massing for Boothman. Evidence of both a tight budget and a high value placed on aesthetics is present in the choice of windows in the house: the small (approximately ten-by-twelve feet) main room has five windows of four different sizes, suggesting that Boothman was using his available stock rather than ordering window units specifically for this house. The actual choice and layout of windows also deviates slightly from Boothman's drawings (in fact, several significant differences exist between finished

J. H. Boothman drawing for Bartlett Cottage (1919), east elevation. Collection of J. H. Boothman.

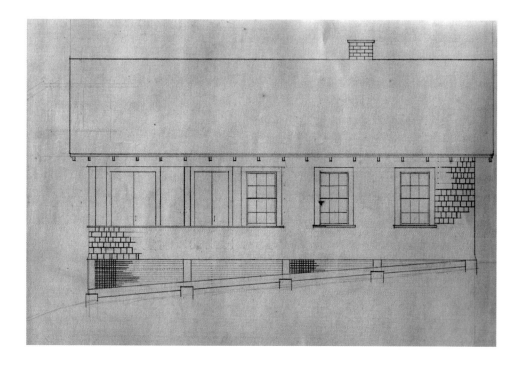

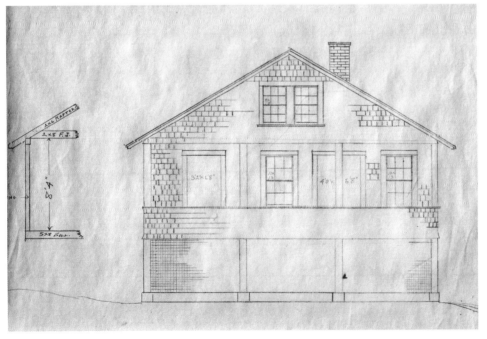

Bartlett Cottage, Randolph, New Hampshire (J. H. Boothman, 1919).

ABOVE: *Exterior, view from south.*

LEFT: *J. H. Boothman drawing for Bartlett Cottage (1919), south elevation. Collection of J. H. Boothman.*

Bartlett Cottage, Randolph, New Hampshire (J. H. Boothman, 1919).

ABOVE: *Main room.*

LEFT: *Main room, door to screened porch, built by Boothman.*

BELOW: *Main door, board and batten, built by Boothman.*

house and the plans). Boothman often fabricated his own interior doors using simple board-and-batten construction; here the main door and French doors leading to the in-cut porch were also built by him. Adjacent to the in-cut porch is a bedroom with a large shuttered bay opening onto the porch; when opened, this very small room, with two other windows opening to the outside, becomes a sleeping porch.

Boothman's style, including his characteristic framing, is apparent throughout the Bartlett cottage. Another distinctive feature present here, and typical not only of Boothman but of most domestic architecture in this period, is the insistence on a certain level of style regardless of budgetary constraints. The large number of windows in the Bartlett house, including four that essentially communicate between interior spaces, would probably not be included in any budget-constrained project of a later period. The presence of light and visual connections between interior spaces and the outdoors remains paramount, a crucial aspect in every summer house, no matter how modest.

Bartlett Cottage, Randolph, New Hampshire (J. H. Boothman, 1919), bedroom convertible to sleeping porch. Hatch windows allowed enclosed rooms to be opened up and more completely exposed to outside breezes than opening windows alone. With the hatch and windows opened, this bedroom was open to the outside on three sides.

DOROTHY YOUNG COTTAGE

*D. Young Cottage, Randolph,
New Hampshire.*

The 1922 Dorothy Young Cottage is a good example of Boothman's fully developed personal style, and one that has suffered only very minimal subsequent alteration. Boothman's ledger records for the Young Cottage are preserved, but no drawings are known. The house may well have been built from an architect's plan – certain details, most particularly a flue serving both stories set at an angle to the framing, suggest another designer provided basic drawings – but the framing and interior finish are, typically and distinctly, in Boothman's style.

Like most of Randolph's summer houses, the Young Cottage is oriented toward the view of the summits of Mts. Adams and Madison to the south, although tall forest surrounds the house today, blocking much of this view. It is built on and approached from a steep south-facing slope, making its appearance difficult to appreciate from outside. The building is laid out with the principal roof gable oriented on an east–west axis with the main rooms and bedrooms all provided with a southerly exposure. The east end of the house is terminated by a north–south oriented gabled ell with a cantilevered second-story bay window, part of the second-floor main bedroom. As with virtually all of Boothman's later houses, the cladding is entirely in cedar shingles with no corner or eave trim, creating the continuous and uniform wall texture typical of the Shingle style. While the massing and roof lines of this house are not Shingle style in its most fully formed sense, the house is nevertheless very much of that period.

Boothman's choice of framing materials determines much of the character of the main room, and since the interior walls are uncovered, the framing itself serves as part of the interior finish. The exposed frame required the use of planed lumber and more meticulous construction than is found in work covered with interior paneling. In Boothman's houses exposed cuts are always precise, and nailing is done carefully,

with no hammer-scarring evident. Boothman also chose large framing members spaced more widely than the typical sixteen-inch spacing used for two-inch framing lumber in balloon or platform framing. These larger, more widely spaced members are a hallmark feature of all of Boothman's later uninsulated houses and influence the lighting of the room and the viewer's perception of depth. The open spaces between studs and joists reduce shadowing and minimally disrupt the uniform planar surfaces of the interior walls. They break up the wall space into sections, emphasizing the scale and depth of the room more than would be accomplished by flat-finished walls. The framing also provides easy attachment points for shelving and built-in bookshelves, although in this case the horizontal nailers are simply used as dish rails. It is unknown to what degree Boothman analyzed his framing in terms of its aesthetic design, but from the evidence of the houses his choices for size and spacing of framing were deliberate and very specific.[25] Although no fixed pattern of timber size and spacing is used throughout his houses, Boothman clearly preferred larger timbers, for the general style of construction shown here is repeated in most of his uninsulated houses.

How much of the Young Cottage was the product of Boothman's own sense of design, and how much came from the client or client's architect? Without a plan or correspondence, there is no way to know positively what Boothman's role was in the design of this house or how he may have balanced aesthetic and practical considerations. The resemblance between this and Boothman's other uninsulated houses, however, argues for his creative control over a large part of the project.

By 1923, Boothman had built a number of houses in a variety of styles in Randolph, and these would have provided a catalog of sorts for potential clients to view while staying as guests at one of the hotels. Long-term summer residents in Randolph frequently spent several summers at one of the town's hotels before building their own house, and their time there would have given them opportunities to view

D. Young Cottage, Randolph,
New Hampshire (J. H. Boothman, 1924).

ABOVE LEFT: *Main door, commercially produced millwork,
48" wide, with panes arranged in
ranks of five over three.*

ABOVE RIGHT: *Front porch.*

RIGHT: *Main bedroom bay
window.*

Boothman's other work and negotiate with him on the purchase of land (most of which Boothman owned) and design and construction. Included in Boothman's papers are correspondence with clients, deed transactions, and house plans from different sources, ranging from commissioned architectural drawings to rough sketches clearly drawn by someone unfamiliar with carpentry or design. Most common among these, however, are plans drawn proficiently by one individual who is an experienced, but not a formally trained, architect – presumably Boothman himself. Some of these are annotated in an unfamiliar hand, requesting changes or adding details, probably notes made by the client on a design originally offered by Boothman. Consistencies of construction among many of Boothman's houses also suggest that he was either the principal designer or had a large degree of autonomy in interior layout and finish, while the differences between houses provide evidence of the individual contributions of clients.

Boothman's use of large and widely spaced exposed framing members strongly suggest aesthetic design decisions on his part but also raise the question of what variety of materials were in fact available to him. Standardized lumber was becoming commonplace by the first decades of the twentieth century but was not universal,

D. Young Cottage, Randolph, New Hampshire (J. H. Boothman, 1924), main room (parlor). The structural framing is exposed and forms a part of the wall finish. Walls are formed by a 5" × 5" spruce top plate supported on 4" × 4" posts on 4' centers. Tongue-and-groove pine paneling is attached to one side of the frame with 2" × 5" nailers at ⅓ and ⅔ height; each interior partition appears as a uniform paneled wall on one side, and a wall broken into bays by the frame on the other side, as seen here. Ceiling joists in this room are 2" × 5" spruce on 24" centers. The joist and post spacing is irregular, varying as much as one inch from one bay to another.

D. Young Cottage, Randolph, New Hampshire (J. H. Boothman, 1924), main bedroom. The main bedroom occupies the south (front façade) aspect of the ell that forms the east end of the house and includes the square bay with four casement windows. In contrast to the parlor, where the partition frame faces into the room, the paneled side of the partition faces in here. The effect of the exposed framing members depends upon the size of the room; in larger rooms the bays provide a sense of scale and perspective but can crowd a smaller room. Here, the uniform paneling gives this small room a more open appearance uncluttered by the frame.

especially in rural areas such as Randolph. Locally produced lumber was abundantly available in a wide variety of sizes and would typically be cut to order for a particular job.[26] Rather than being limited to available stock material, Boothman could have ordered framing material cut and planed to his specification, albeit at additional expense. In those houses where framing was conventionally covered,[27] however, Boothman used rough-cut lumber in stock sizes and spacing. His choice of unique sizes for exposed framing materials was thus dictated neither by availability nor reduced expense, while its appearance in all of his later exposed frame houses suggests that it was Boothman's aesthetic sense that sustained his interest in its use.

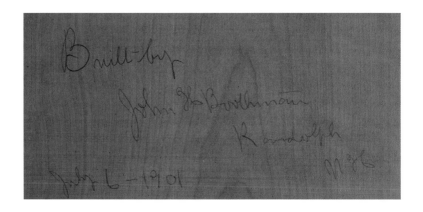

John H. Boothman's signature

The West Side of the Mountains

In the 1840s, the White Mountains were an austere and wild subject for painters, and by the 1870s they had become an alpine wonderland for intrepid hikers and trailbuilders. Late in the eighteenth century, however, they were principally a formidable and inconvenient barrier to transportation and commerce between coastal New England and the growing farm communities along the Coös Intervales on the upper Connecticut River. In the late 1700s, the Connecticut River was the principal (although not easily navigated) access to northern New Hampshire and Vermont from points to the south in central Massachusetts and Connecticut, but the river offered no useful access from the major coastal commercial centers further northeast in Boston and Portland, Maine. Communities in northern New Hampshire and Vermont needed to get their products to distant markets; businesses on the coast were eager to sell to a new and growing market on the far side of the mountains, and neither could be accomplished without efficient access through the White Mountains.

The "Notch of the White Mountains" (or Crawford Notch, as it is known today) was found in 1771 by Lancaster resident Timothy Nash while tracking a moose. It bore faint traces of an Indian trail, and in 1775, following a grant made by Governor John Wentworth to Nash and Benjamin Sawyer, a rough road was established through the Notch. Among the early residents of the Notch and the valley immediately to the northwest were the Crawfords, who, starting in 1790, built homesteads and later operated guest houses both south of the Notch (at Bemis) and beyond the Notch's northwestern end, at the location known today as Fabyan's. The Willeys also came into the Notch around this time, the first of that line building a house in 1793 on the site where, in 1826, the family would be buried in the famous landslide by which they are now memorialized.

The rough road through the Notch became a well-traveled trade route and the early accommodations offered by the Crawfords and Willeys were commercially successful. Continued population increase and economic growth in the Coös Intervales spurred further improvements to access through the mountains, and in 1803 the state chartered a road to be constructed north from Bartlett through the Notch to the towns of Coös County. This road, the Tenth New Hampshire Turnpike, was to have been part of a much longer road connecting Portland with Lake Champlain; plans to complete the connections to the east and west faltered, but the Crawford Notch road was an immediate success. The *History of Coös County* describes the traffic on the road in those early days:

> *Until the advent of the railroad, this was the great outlet of Coös County, and the thoroughfare over which its merchandise came from Portland. In winter often, lines of teams from Coös, over half a mile in length, might be seen going down with tough Canadian*

horses harnessed to pungs or sleighs, loaded with pot or pearl ash, butter, cheese, pork, lard and peltry, returning with well assorted loads of merchandise.[28]

Following the publicity accompanying the death of the Willey family in the great storm and landslide of August 1826, the Notch immediately became a widely known destination for tourists and artists, a market that the Crawfords worked hard to develop.

Ethan Allen Crawford served guests at his tavern and lodgings at Fabyan's, near present-day Bretton Woods, while his brother Thomas and father Abel, ran popular lodging places at the very head of the Notch and eight miles further south at Bemis. Commercial interest in the route remained the principal motivation for continued investment in the road through this precipitous gap, however, with repairs to the road following the 1826 storm being financed in part by Portland businessmen. Crawford Notch remained an important artery for commerce for the next century, especially following the construction of the Portland and Ogdensberg Railroad in 1875. This line connected Portland, Maine, to Fabyan's at the head of Crawford Notch, following the first half of the route conceived by the planners of the Tenth New Hampshire Turnpike. At Fabyan's, the line connected with the Boston, Concord, and Montreal Railroad, whose lines served the communities of Woodsville, Bath, Lisbon, Littleton, Bethlehem, Jefferson, Lancaster, and points further west in Vermont. The Coös Intervales and surrounding areas previously isolated by the White Mountains were finally fully connected to the coast and the population centers to the southeast, not only at a time of great potential for growth in manufacturing, trade, and agriculture, but as tourism, with its romantic and sublime origins mingled with the debris of the Willey Slide, was taking its place as New England's next golden opportunity.

BETHLEHEM AND SYLVANUS D. MORGAN

The town of Bethlehem, chartered in 1799, lay in the path of the commercial traffic that flowed in and out through the narrow gap at Crawford Notch. A tavern, licensed to resident Lot Woodward by the town's newly minted selectmen, was Bethlehem's first accommodation for travelers. Bethlehem's location, not only near the intersection of important commercial routes but also on a hill with a fine distant vantage of the Presidential Range, turned out to be the making of the town's fortune.

The early decades of Bethlehem's growth depended on the commercial traffic moving back and forth between Portland and the Coös Intervales, and a variety of businesses, including lodgings for travelers, sprang up to supplement the farming and logging which were the community's origins. The beauty of Bethlehem's surroundings evidently had an effect even on stern New England commercial travelers:

Sylvanus D. Morgan (1857–1940).

The everlasting hills among which this village had been built began to assert them-
selves . . . and from the line of travelers passing daily through Bethlehem an occasional
straggler fell from the ranks for a few days' sojourn in the midst of so much enchantment.
These few had before long become many, and simultaneous with the town's decline in a
commercial sense came a new importance: Bethlehem was a watering-place.[29]

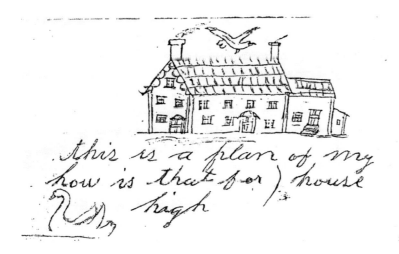

Excerpt from letter, S. D. Morgan,
1876.

The main event which pushed Bethlehem toward its future as a summer resort
occurred in 1863 when Rhode Island lawyer (and later governor) Henry Howard
recuperated from injuries sustained in a carriage accident at the Sinclair House, one
of Bethlehem's first hotels. Howard was so impressed by Bethlehem and its climate,
which he believed to possess an "uncommon potency for health,"[30] that he bought
two farms in town that he subdivided and sold as building lots, offering financial
assistance to entrepreneurs who would start hotels. In 1871, Boston businessman
Issac Cruft followed Howard's example, buying land that he developed into the
Maplewood Hotel – one of Bethlehem's largest and most famous establishments.

Energetic promotion by the publisher of the *White Mountain Echo* (a popular summertime weekly periodical published in Bethlehem starting in 1878) and the choice
of Bethlehem for the headquarters of the American Hay Fever Association spread the
town's fame as a summer resort. The clientele who came here were appreciative of the
beauty of the White Mountains as viewed from Bethlehem (along with the climate,
one of the town's principal assets) but generally were not seeking rustic experiences
like fishing or hiking to the degree that visitors to Rangeley or Randolph sought.
Bethlehem became very widely known, however, for healthful air, beauty, and comfort. In 1880 some seventeen hotels were operating in Bethlehem, and by the early
twentieth century the town was the most highly developed resort destination in the
White Mountains, with accommodations for as many as 2,000 guests.

Such an extensive building boom required architects, carpenters, and capable
and efficient contractors able to manage large projects, given the large scale of some

Glass doorknob, Upland Cottage, Bethlehem, New Hampshire (S. D. Morgan, 1916). Morgan used these distinctive crystal globes as a decorative motif on doors, cabinets, and drawers throughout the house.

of the hotels. Among the many builders and designers responsible for creating the infrastructure of the White Mountain tourist industry, Sylvanus D. Morgan (1857–1940) is the best known and possibly the most prolific. Morgan was very well known in his day, and, unlike the other builders whose work is shown in this book, he remains so today. His story has been told elsewhere,[31] but it is worth retelling here briefly, for the unusual circumstances of his early life and education place Morgan very squarely in the category of highly talented, self-taught vernacular builders.

Sylvanus D. Morgan was born in 1857 in Weld, Maine. By the age of fourteen, his mother and all of his siblings had succumbed to tuberculosis, and Morgan, orphaned, set off on foot to join relatives living in Hooksett, New Hampshire, 200 miles to the south. Morgan completed his schooling at Hookset and found work in a sawmill, but, possibly due to his fears of his own susceptibility to tuberculosis, he moved sometime before 1880 to Bethlehem, already widely known for its beneficial fresh air. Morgan had shown an interest in building at an early age – a letter he wrote in 1876 to a cousin in Weld includes a drawing depicting "a plan of my house" – and by the 1880 census, he was listed as a resident of Bethlehem employed as a carpenter.

From these difficult beginnings, Morgan advanced rapidly to become a highly proficient builder, aware of popular architectural styles and very capable (on the evidence of the many buildings of his still extant today) of designing and constructing houses and hotels in a wide variety of styles. He is known to have worked on Bethlehem's Sinclair House in 1883, at age twenty-six, and to have built the Elmwood House in Franconia (possibly his first project as an independent contractor) in the following year, subsequently managing it until it burned in 1889. While in Franconia he met and married Kathryn George. After the loss of the Elmwood House, they moved to Lisbon, which remained their home until Morgan's death in 1940. From his shops in Lisbon, Morgan supervised an enormous number of projects throughout the White Mountains ranging from moderately sized summer houses to large hotels, including the second Profile House in Franconia Notch. His projects also included a school and commercial blocks in Lisbon, both the second Tip-Top House and the third Summit House on Mt. Washington, major additions to the Balsams in Dixville Notch, and North Conway's Memorial Hospital.

Sylvanus Morgan worked extensively with the hotel developer Frank H. Abbott, and later with Abbott's son, Karl, both in New Hampshire, where Frank Abbott owned and operated the Upland Hotel, and in Florida, where the Abbott family owned several other hotels.[32] Morgan received several of his early opportunities to build large projects through his association with the Abbotts and may have gained much of his wide exposure to architectural trends and styles through them as well. One of the most striking demonstrations of Morgan's awareness of and talent for contemporary architecture was his design and construction of Upland Cottage (1915–1916) in Bethlehem, built for Frank Abbott's son, Karl, as a wedding present from the parents of his bride, Florence Ivie. Upland Cottage is a polished and masterfully executed Craftsman-style house, constructed to a very high standard both structurally and ornamentally. Morgan was not building for the same clientele as John Boothman and the many builders like Boothman who built imaginatively on a typically small scale. Morgan built imaginatively on a large scale (most especially in his hotels, of course), using fine materials and extensive finish and detail work. Upland Cottage is massive for a Craftsman-style structure, both in style and actual construction. Built on a full basement, winterized, the interior finished with fine hardwood cabinetry and paneling, and showing a graceful heaviness in its roof lines and massing, Upland Cottage was not intended to be a summer camp or cottage expressive of a departure from routine and a temporary intimacy with nature. It was, instead, a meticulous and expert example of an urbane style still near the height of its popularity[33] – an appropriate house for the Abbotts, a family with high standing in the community and in the hotel business. The fact that Upland Cottage was built immediately adjacent to Frank Abbott's Upland Hotel probably provided additional reasons to build an attractive and stylish building, further evidence of comfort and sophistication to be seen by hotel clients who for the most part were not seeking a rustic vacation experience.

Upland Cottage has been discussed in other studies of New England architecture, but while Morgan is definitely known to have built Upland Cottage (one of many summer houses Morgan built in Bethlehem), the origins of its design were

Upland Cottage, Bethlehem, New Hampshire (S. D. Morgan, 1916), view from east.

unclear. In addition to Morgan himself, various architects, including the California architects Greene and Greene, have been proposed as the building's designer. Drawings kept at Morgan's home of fifty-seven years, examined in 2008, include a single sheet drawn in Morgan's hand (his drawing style is well-established from other complete drawings) showing the window layout and framing for the second-floor porch located above the front door on Upland Cottage. This fragment, showing that Morgan designed a significant framing element of the original structure, provides virtually certain proof that Morgan was in fact Upland Cottage's architect as well as its builder, and reinforces his well-deserved reputation as one of New Hampshire's most talented and highly accomplished builders during the state's growth as a recreational destination.

Upland Cottage, Bethlehem, New Hampshire (S. D. Morgan, 1916).

RIGHT: *Drawing for Upland Cottage construction (S. D. Morgan, 1916). M. McKeever collection, Lisbon, New Hampshire. This drawing, found among a collection of drawings at Morgan's home (from 1891 to 1948) in Lisbon, New Hampshire, shows the framing layout for the second-floor porch above the main entrance of Upland Cottage.*

OPPOSITE, TOP: *Living room.*

OPPOSITE, BOTTOM: *Dining room.*

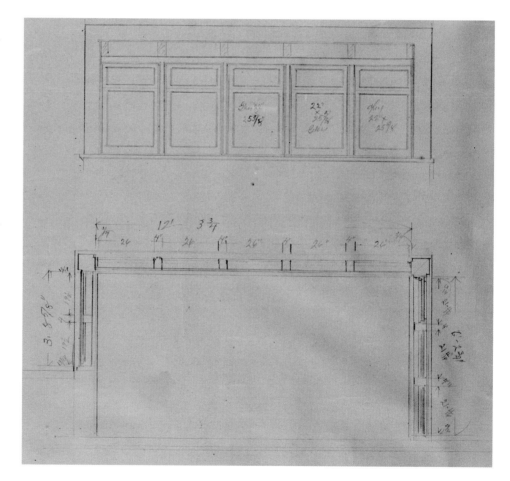

Caspian Lake, Greensboro, Vermont.

VERMONT

The porch of the Big House overlooks a lot of family history.
Wallace Stegner, *Crossing to Safety*

CASPIAN LAKE, in Greensboro, Vermont, is a beautiful place today and must have been even more so in the days when farmers kept the surrounding hills cleared for crops and feed for cattle. Even at the time of the region's first surveys in the 1790s, however, when then unnamed Caspian Lake was still surrounded by the original primeval wilderness, it must have left a strong impression, for the earliest maps[1] identify it as Beautiful Lake. The lake is small, about a mile and a half long, very deep, and its waters are exceptionally clear. The hills of the Northeast Kingdom countryside roll gently down to the lake's shores, giving views of Mt. Mansfield to the west and the White Mountains to the east. This landscape is not mountainous or wild; it is essentially pastoral, different in character from the austere, unbridled energy of New Hampshire's high mountains or Maine's ocean coast. It is a country shaped by people for 200 years.

Greensboro owes its long history as a community to a road: the Bayley–Hazen military road, which cut across northern Vermont from Newbury on the Connecticut River toward Canada in the late 1770s. The end of the French and Indian War in 1763 opened the door to settlement of the remoter areas of northern Vermont, but military conflicts were by no means over. By 1776 the enemy had become the British, who staged their northern campaigns from Canada. Construction of the Bayley–Hazen road was begun in that year, following a proposal by Col. Jacob Bayley of Newbury to Gen. George Washington that a road would speed the moving of men and supplies north toward the enemy's encampments. As it happened, the road was never completed for that purpose – circumstances eventually changed, and it became clear that the road might serve England's purposes better than America's – but the portion of the road that was built passed through Greensboro, connecting it to the region's main artery of eighteenth-century settlement, the Connecticut River. Greensboro itself was chartered in 1781, its boundaries surveyed, and lots

Kayaks on Caspian Lake, Greensboro, Vermont.

assigned to sixty-eight named proprietors. From that time on, Greensboro was no longer a part of the wilderness but of the world of men, civilization, and the slow and methodical progress of the eighteenth and early nineteenth centuries.

A great part of the aesthetic appeal of Greensboro, and northern New England in general, lies in the juxtaposition of its natural beauty with its built environment. The words "pastoral" and "picturesque" are not out of place here. By no means does all of Vermont fit the quaint stereotype: the neat village green, the white, steepled church, flaming red maples bounded by an ancient stone wall. But a surprising number of places do fit, or fit some variation, of that stereotype, especially in comparison with other parts of the United States where progress happened later, faster, and with bigger tools. The enterprising settlers of Greensboro in the last decade of the eighteenth century and the first decades of the nineteenth century might have been, in their beliefs and habits, no better custodians of their environment, no wiser in their ability to take the long view, than their counterparts in the American West a hundred years later. But they were bound by their technology and resources to build their environment on a more intimate scale and in far greater harmony with the natural landscape. Such resources as nature offered had to be used efficiently where they appeared. Homes, businesses, and farms needed to be close together because transportation was difficult. Roads had to follow the contours of the land, and rivers had to have their full potential for transportation and power utilized. And this development happened (in comparison to future events) slowly.

This is not to say that Vermont or rural New England in general was spared the devastation of progress. The stumpage on the ground following New Hampshire's first major logging operations, Maine's rivers in the dirty days of pulp and paper production, or the holes and craters torn in Vermont's landscape by mining and quarrying bore witness to that. Most of those scars are gone today. In many cases the New England climate simply allowed the landscape to heal faster than it would in, say, Nevada.

Walking among the hills of Vershire now, fifty miles south of Greensboro and equally pastoral, one finds no hint (save a small fenced-in Superfund site) of the treeless wasteland created there by the Ely copper mine 120 years before. But most of these devastations came later, borne on the powerful and impatient shoulders of machines and technology into a landscape already arranged according to the needs and abilities of its earliest settlers. The basic imprint of the eighteenth century has, in many parts of northern New England, somehow survived, and this largely due to the human values still active in these places today. Greensboro offered both its residents and its summer visitors continuity, knowledge of its past, and a sense of harmony with landscape and time.

In 1879, when the first long-term summer campers arrived, the town of Greensboro was a small, well-established commercial center, accessible by railroad (harbinger of the industrial world but comparatively benign at that time) and occupied by a diverse and capable permanent population, nearly twice the size of today's, engaged in a variety of agricultural and manufacturing activities.[2] The lake was surrounded by farmland but was itself of value to residents principally as a source of water for Greensboro's several mills and as a source of ice in winter. Farmers whose lands abutted the lakeshore willingly sold parcels to campers, although they might continue to mow hay in the camper's fields in exchange for some additional service such as cutting and storing ice for the camper's summer use. Benjamin H. Sanborn,

Caspian Lake, Greensboro, Vermont.

a publisher of high school textbooks and early Caspian summer resident, bought land on the lake's south shore from farmer Henry Tolman, whose ancestors were among the proprietors listed on Greensboro's 1781 charter. Sanborn, having potential customers for land sales in his academic clients, subdivided his land; thus Caspian's first summer community included many academics — a characteristic that persists today. The original group of summer camps was known as the Randolph camps after founder Avery Wheeler's wintertime residence in Randolph, Vermont, and was built on land purchased from Sanborn. These were true camps. As at many other summer colonies, they were initially canvas tents on wooden platforms serving as houses and were often accompanied by a simple one-room kitchen. Houses in a variety of sizes and types followed, but Caspian's summer colony architecture was, and remains, simple and unobtrusive, like the lake that remains its aesthetic focus.

GEORGE D. FOWLER

Greensboro builder George D. Fowler (1867–1942).

Among Greensboro's many tradesmen and artisans were, of course, carpenters. Aaron Hill, son of Peleg Hill, another one of Greensboro's original proprietors, was the town's first builder, and some of his houses still stand and are occupied today. By the 1870s, more than a dozen builders, woodworkers, and masons were employed in Greensboro. The most widely known may have been the Perrin brothers, Lester and Alden, woodworker and metalworker, respectively, who built and sold products ranging from butter boxes to carriages. For the summer residents, however, the greatest of the house builders was George D. Fowler. Fowler built more than forty houses around Caspian Lake, most of which stand today. As did Boothman in Randolph and Norwood in Southwest Harbor, Fowler would build from architect's plans or from his own designs, often adapting features he encountered in architectural drawings to his own future use. For a builder so widely renowned in the community, surprisingly little is known about Fowler's background and personal life. His place of birth, education, and his life before coming to Greensboro are unknown. He had no family and lived in rented rooms in town. He is buried in the Greensboro cemetery, and his headstone provides no further clues beyond the dates of his birth and death: 13 June 1867–28 February 1942. His life is still fresh in the memories of some current Greensboro residents, and glimpses of his character and building practices can be picked out.[3]

Fowler was, first and foremost, highly respected and honored for his work. Summer resident Arthur Perry in 1977 recalled Fowler as someone "who took a tremendous pride in his work and was one of the most aristocratic persons I have ever known."[4] Lacie Smith, who as a teenager worked for Fowler for two summers late in his career in the 1930s, described Fowler as operating at that time with a very small crew and as being easygoing and very independent in his plans and decisions

Fern Ledges, Caspian Lake, Greensboro, Vermont (additions made by G. D. Fowler).

ABOVE: *Note the Shingle style aspects of this house: extensive but irregular and multiple roof lines, continuous shingle cladding, without trim boards at eaves or corners, extending even to the pillars supporting the porch. Imagine the house with only a few changes, however: replace the shingle cladding by white clapboards, remove the wraparound porch and perhaps remove the hipped roof on the right-hand side – the house becomes a traditional New England farmhouse.*

RIGHT: *Screen porch, lake view.*

about buildings and renovation. Fowler's independence was confirmed by another resident, whose parents' summer house he renovated one fall and winter in the 1930s, modifying their request and raising the house, on his own initiative and without their knowledge, a full story. Fowler's judgment as a builder, however idiosyncratic, was respected. Arthur Perry made this further comment: "Nobody was treated with the deference that George Fowler was."

There are no papers, no plans, no family to tell us more about George Fowler, except for a poem, written by a Caspian summer resident some years ago. We have his houses, however, and in those we can see the work of an inventive, aesthetically attentive mind, attuned not only to the needs and desires of his clients but to the presence of the landscape – the lake – and to the reasons one would choose, either for a summer or a lifetime, to live in such a place.

Fern Ledges, Caspian Lake, Greensboro, Vermont (additions made by G. D. Fowler).

ABOVE LEFT: *Upstairs corridor and bedroom. The size of this house allows for a more generous allocation of space to corridors, and this second-floor hall has been placed against an outside wall and given a window.*

ABOVE RIGHT: *Roof framing detail. Compare this view to the bedroom at Keystone Cottage in East Boothbay, Maine. Here again, portions of the roof framing have been deliberately exposed and others sheathed to reveal the supporting structure of the house along with finished surfaces.*

OPPOSITE: *Main room. Oversized joists allow a wide ceiling span; wall studding is covered in pine paneling in this case.*

THE CARPENTER

He'd never known the plans of an architect.
Our homemade sketches, the old carpenter
Transformed into a cottage, sound and trim.
We often came to watch him and his men,
Their tools "hand-powered," rafter cuts by eye.
At work, they seldom spoke, but toward lunchtime
His pale blue eyes would crinkle a slow smile,
His long mustaches — white, tobacco stained —
Would twitch with humor. "You c'n fall th' brass
Right top that dinnerpail." From off the stump,
Its owner snatched it just in time.
He rose
From his sawhorses, the tall frame
Bowed permanently — from the work he did,
Bent over saws. And age. And shy reserve.
When lunch was done, he filled his gamy pipe,
Leaned back against the shingle bales, and spoke
In mild unhurried tones: "A fella come
From over St. J. once, tried sellin' me
Some fancy shingles. Told him bucket o' lime
Is jes' as good. You spill it 'long th' ridgepole.
Rain'll wash it down 'n' spread her even.
Shingle keep fur years. I've tore a lot off,
Down below th' chimney, good as new
'Count of all th' lime come washin' out th' bricks."
He stroked his always-three-day-stubbled chin.
"So I begun t' put lime crost th' roof."
At work again, he saw our questioning gaze.
"Them collagirds, we had t' lay up wet.

Look dirty till they dry. If we'd a tried
to clean 'em, dirt'd jest a-grindled in."
When afternoon wore on to quitting time,
He drawled: "You fellas c'n leave any time
Now, you've a mind to, but I'm goin' home."
And "home" to him was where we called on him next year
To thank him for his masterwork. His home,
A lonely room in someone else's house
Beside him at his turkey carpet chair,
His hound dog nuzzled in his master's lap.
"A great dog to be made of," and he smiled
Affectionately sad, for this hound-dog was new. . .
His favorite had been poisoned in the fall.
"No, not a-purpose," and he held the match
Unheeded at his pipe-bowl till it died.
"A fella's horse down river way took sick.
Vet give it poison. Left it top th' ground.
Two-three dogs poisoned by it. My old Jim
Tried gettin' home. He dropped 'fore he got here."

"Why do you think George Fowler gets new dogs?
His hunting days are over, so he says."
"You saw the way he held and scratched that head
Right in his lap. He's got to have a dog.
He must be really lonely there sometimes. . .
And always building other people's homes."

PHILIP GRAY,
from *Greensboro Remembers: Poems for the Bicentennial.*
Northlight Studio Press, Barre, Vermont, 1976.

Barr Outlook, Caspian Lake, Greensboro, Vermont (G. D. Fowler). This house was built by Fowler from plans purchased from House Beautiful Publishing Co. The exterior follows the drawing faithfully.

Barr Outlook

Despite the assertion in Philip Gray's poem, George Fowler did occasionally work from architect's drawings. Barr Outlook was built by Fowler, with some modifications, from plans drawn for the owner by *House Beautiful* magazine's "Home Builder Service Bureau." The house as built differs from its plan in some significant respects (the flat-roofed portico on the northwest elevation, for example, has been replaced by a more weather-resistant hipped roof), but more significantly, no specific details were given for interior finish, and Fowler, like Boothman in Randolph, adopted a framing plan better suited for exposure as interior walls than a conventional framing plan would have been. Fowler's selection of timber sizes and spacing is strikingly similar to Boothman's choices in (for example) the Brickelmeyer and Young cottages.

Like the more widely known *Ladies' Home Journal, House Beautiful* was directed to a readership of home owners, mostly women, rather than builders, and published articles on house planning, furnishing, and decorating, all of which promoted Progressive ideals of domesticity, aesthetics, health, and efficiency. By the 1930s, when this plan was drawn, the era of the magazine's involvement in actual architectural services was near its end, and the reforms of the Progressive movement[5] had been assimilated, in domestic architecture at least. The Craftsman style and its subtype, the Bungalow, embodied this assimilation; just around the corner was a new era in American domestic architecture, already being explored by modernists like Richard Neutra.

Barr Outlook, Caspian Lake, Greensboro, Vermont (G. D. Fowler).

ABOVE: *Main room. The built-in shelves and unusual fireplace, the brick placed flush with paneling, were Fowler's design, and not specified in the drawings.*

RIGHT: *Plan drawn by House Beautiful Publishing Co., 1931.*

BELOW: *Window seat and built-in bookshelves.*

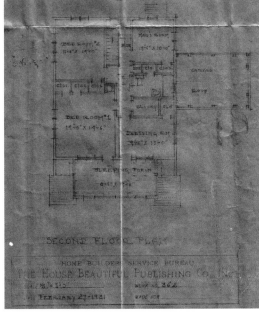

NOBILITAT AND TRUE NORTH

True North, Caspian Lake, Greensboro, Vermont (G. D. Fowler). Built in 1908 by Fowler from plans provided by a Philadelphia architect, True North derives its bungalow character in part from the continuity of the roof line joining the house and wrap-around porch.

Nobilitat and True North are two adjacent houses built for the same family by George Fowler. Fowler built Nobilitat in 1905 from his own designs; True North, built in 1908, was constructed from plans drawn by a Philadelphia architect whose name is now unknown.

True North is a compact two-story house with an approximately square plan, surrounded on three sides by a veranda. The veranda roof line is continuous with the main roof, creating a bungalow-like profile. Shingle-style influences are also evident in the roofline, in the continuous shingle cladding, and in the second-story dormers. The central five-sided dormer dominates the roof line and from inside gives an excellent view of the lake.

True North's ground floor is divided into three rooms but has no interior bearing walls; the entire second story is carried by a system of stacked rafters. Perimeter bearing walls and a central stairwell support crossed 9″ × 5½″ purlins that in turn carry 6½″ × 2½″ second-story floor joists. This method of supporting the upper story is simple and strong but raises the height of the ground floor the height of the purlins (nine inches in this case). The added height doesn't affect the appearance of the interior since the apparent ceiling height is fixed by the lower surfaces of the crossed purlins. Purlins carrying roof rafters are quite common, especially in log and heavy timber construction, but less so when used to carry floor joists (although the same framing is visible in the Levi Hallowell and William Allen house in Ocean

Nobilitat, Caspian Lake, Greensboro, Vermont (G. D. Fowler). Compare the symmetry of this house to that of its companion, True North.

Point, Maine). The use of interlocking timbers creates an intricate but not busy construction, while details like chamfered edges on the purlins offset what might otherwise be a very heavy and massive appearance.

The second floor contains a bathroom and four bedrooms, with partition walls separating the bedrooms only up to the level of the eaves. Like Camp Kennebago at Rangeley, privacy was not a paramount concern in the design of this house, and like so many of the summer houses seen here, the details and finish of the second story, normally a private family space, are much simpler and more rustic than the more public ground floor. Eliminating the ceiling saves costs and allows greater air circulation under the uninsulated roof – although the design typically results in uncomfortably hot nights in warm, calm conditions.

The unnamed architect of True North struck a successful balance here between the intimate shelter of a small cottage and the more robust and imposing character of timber frame construction. This same balance is present in the Craftsman style and its derivative, the Bungalow, but in 1908, the year of True North's construction, these styles were just emerging; in another decade they would be enormously popular across the United States. True North is transitional, taller in its roof line than Craftsman styles would become (in part because of the stacked rafters), and, under its wide veranda, nearly a Cape Cod in its general shape.

Nobilitat, the earlier of the two houses, and Fowler's own creation (presumably with general guidance from the family), is (like Boothman's Wollaston Lodge and Thornbush) an amalgam, with rustic elements (uninterrupted shingle cladding, exposed rafter

Nobilitat, Caspian Lake, Greensboro, Vermont (G. D. Fowler).

ABOVE: *Main room. While the room is very simple in form and finish, Fowler created a prominent ornamental setting for the fireplace.*

LEFT: *Fowler frequently used this "Frame-in-Frame" motif in which one structure – a fireplace, cabinet, or porch element – is surrounded by a frame which plays no obvious structural role but sets off the inner element visually.*

OPPOSITE: *True North, Caspian Lake, Greensboro, Vermont (G. D. Fowler).*

TOP: *Main room.*

LEFT: *Bedroom.*

RIGHT: *Bathroom. The prominent five-sided dormer seen from outside is, surprisingly, the bathroom. This room, tucked into a back corner or otherwise isolated in the vast majority of houses, is in fact one of the most heavily used shared spaces in any house. Viewed in this way, this bathroom's very attractive setting makes perfect sense.*

ends, chalet-like decorative shutters) applied to a very regular and symmetrical plan with (rather distant) antecedents in Post-Colonial and Colonial Revival styles. Nobilitat's interior is simply proportioned and has one feature in common with True North: a purlin supporting the second story floor joists. The design here is more primitive and camp-like than at True North (compare the framing and sheathing of the main room walls in both houses, for example), but Fowler built in a number of explicitly ornamental details, including screen-like devices surrounding the fireplace and a large dish closet. These ornaments are repeated in a few of Fowler's other houses, and share with True North's stacked rafters the character of a "frame-within-a-frame." There is not enough information to determine if this motif was Fowler's own invention, but in any case he appears to have adopted and applied it at a number of Caspian houses.

Caspian Lake, Greensboro, Vermont (G. D. Fowler), built-in bench.

BANCROFT COTTAGE

Edward Bancroft had his summer house, Bramblewood, built for himself and his daughter, Jesse Hubbell Bancroft,[6] in 1908 at what was formerly a cabin and tent site on the lakeside. The Bancroft Cottage does not appear to have been built from an architect's plan, and shows strong Adirondack Style influence in details but not in overall plan and layout. A massive chimney, log-framed sleeping porch, exposed log roof rafters, and a small and graceful stickwork stair banister all display the Adirrondack style, but the house is comparatively tall in its proportion in comparison to the classic Adirondack lodge. Again, purlins support the second-story rafters, allowing the main room on the ground floor to span the entire width of the house. The framing throughout is extraordinarily heavy (note the size of the roof rafter visible in one of the upstairs bedrooms); this is possibly a part of the Adirondack influence but must also reflect the comparatively low cost of lumber at that time, as well as the ease with which builders could obtain lumber sawn to any particular size.

The Bancroft Cottage is not positively Fowler's work, but its design elements

Bramblewood, Caspian Lake, Greensboro, Vermont (G. D. Fowler), main entrance. This cottage has many of the external details of the Adirondack Lodge, but the massing of the house – high and square – is reminiscent of European masonry designs.

decidedly point to him. Taken collectively, the houses at Caspian Lake, whether built by George Fowler or not, show a wide variety of styles united in large degree by "northern" influences: most are moderately heavy to very heavy in construction, dark in color, and fit well with the forest and lake setting. Caspian Lake shares a type of rustic atmosphere with Randolph, New Hampshire, somewhere between Rangeley, Maine, where a more deliberately rustic camp style prevailed, and the Maine coast, where earlier and more ornamental styles like Queen Anne and formal Shingle style prevailed. Connecting all these styles – at the ocean, on lakes, or in the mountains – is a consistent theme of simple utility combined with modest domestic comfort and grace. The houses present a kind of "functional aesthetic," in which the occupant's experience and activity is of paramount importance, especially the occupant's interaction with the house's natural setting.

Bramblewood (Bancroft Cottage), Caspian Lake, Greensboro, Vermont (G. D. Fowler).

RIGHT: *Main room. The large socially oriented main room, common not only to most vacation houses but to virtually all designs flowing out of the Shingle style, Arts-and-Crafts, and Craftsman movements, depends on ceiling framing that permits wide, unsupported spans. The spans here are accomplished not by purlins, as at Fowler's Nobilitat and True North houses, but by heavy beams spanning the room, with joists to support the upstairs floors mortised into the beams.*

BELOW RIGHT: *Main room of the adjacent guest house. The more conventional studding layout of this room gives it a more unfinished appearance than rooms in the main house despite being essentially no different in the choice of materials or degree of finish.*

Bramblewood (Bancroft Cottage), Caspian Lake, Greensboro, Vermont (G. D. Fowler)

ABOVE: *Staircase. This stickwork banister and rail is a simple detail but is a dramatic presence in the room. Like the staircase in the William Osgood house at Silver Lake, the staircase here depends on this expansive gesture to connect the house's two floors.*

RIGHT: *Sleeping porch. The Adirondack influence is especially clear on this side of the house, which faces out onto the lake.*

White House, Caspian Lake, Greensboro, Vermont (G. D. Fowler).

ABOVE: *After a remodeling job when the owners were away, George Fowler left a note saying simply, "All done – I hope you like it."*

RIGHT: *Passageway between main room and dining room.*

Unnamed cottage at Caspian Lake, Greensboro, Vermont (G. D. Fowler).

ABOVE: *Kitchen. This kitchen was built for use by the house's owners rather than by the servants, and it faces the lake, opening onto the same porch as the main room.*

LEFT: *Main room with folding and sliding exterior doors. Very large doors provided ventilation in summer. As summer houses have become three-season and year-round vacation homes, features like these doors, which are exceptionally difficult to seal and insulate, have disappeared. On hot summer days, however, there is nothing better.*

Mounts Adams and Madison, the northern limit of the Presidential
Range, from Randolph, New Hampshire.

EPILOGUE

I N HIS ESSAY "The Architecture of the American Summer: The Flowering of the Shingle Style,"[1] Vincent Scully conceded that the Shingle style enjoyed a lifetime that extended past 1887, when the architectural profession moved its gaze away from it and back to the more restrained and academic models of the Colonial Revival. He acknowledged that "having entered into the mainstream of the American tradition of domestic building, [the Shingle style] never really ended at all." But Scully's attention remained fixed on theory and on new developments in architecture, so the style's absorption into vernacular tradition was of little interest to him (and subsequently to others), and, far from seeing that absorption as a productive or creative development, he believed that the Shingle style "did not . . . so much die out as, in dwindled and impoverished form, slide below the conscious interest of the profession into the general mass of vernacular building." Nothing in this evolution caught the eye of the architectural profession again until, in the late 1950s, the end of the thread was plucked up out of the general mass by a new generation of designers led by Scully's own favorite, Robert Venturi.

If I have accomplished anything in presenting the houses shown in this book, I hope I have made a convincing case that the architecture of the latter nineteenth century survived into the twentieth century as an admittedly dwindling vernacular form, but not as an impoverished one. The small houses that appeared on the fringes of the great architectural events of the northeast in those days were, in my view, wonderfully creative adaptations of larger buildings, adapted to the desires and resources of a middle class who sought to create an environment closely related aesthetically to the environments conceived by H. H. Richardson, McKim, Mead and White, or John Calvin Stevens. That they were conceived and built (for the most part) not by architects but by local builders trained in craft and guided only by trade literature and their own sensibility makes the houses that much more interesting to me for what they reveal to us about the character, knowledge, and aesthetic sensibilities of a class of craftsmen who, as much or more than their houses did, slipped below the conscious interest of the profession.

These small houses are remarkable not just for their diminished scale but for

ABOVE LEFT: *William Kent House, Tuxedo Park, New York (Bruce Price, 1885).*

ABOVE RIGHT: *Lewis Cottage, Randolph, New Hampshire (J. H. Boothman).*

their distillation of specific qualities originally defined in more elaborate terms by the architectural profession in the 1870s and 1880s. Much of the essence of what McKim, Mead, and White accomplished with all the training, tools, and resources at their disposal, Boothman, Fowler, and Norwood accomplished with plain sawn lumber. Look at Bruce Price's William Kent House (Tuxedo Park, New York, 1885) and compare it to Boothman's Lewis Cottage. The scale is diminished, but where is Scully's impoverishment?

The small-town builders worked at the scale their clients required, but brought to their work the crucial qualities of massing, proportion, and articulation, the entire plan guided by a firm knowledge of the building's purpose and meaning for its occupants. The distillation of the Shingle style as well as other seminal types has been pursued at length since Venturi's earliest days. A generation of architects following Venturi – including, among others, Edward Larrabee Barnes, David Salmela, and Susan Susanka – have pursued small scales and intimate connections to landscape, although in many cases the distillation has been pursued nearly to extinction, the advances of the nineteenth century having subsequently been pressed through the strainer of modernism and the International Style. Nevertheless, I think that the old vernacular descendants – the camps and cottages – still contain new lessons for us: designs that are compact, economical, and aesthetically whole.

The builders were not the only creators and adapters – in some cases, as at Rangeley, Belgrade, and particularly at Squam, the campers themselves established styles rooted in vernacular traditions untapped by the architectural profession at the time, some of which were later adopted by architects and brought to a wider audience through commissioned designs. The building style originating in Rangeley (at least) and interpreted at

Squam in a deliberately primitive fashion created a working definition of "camp": a dwelling created from the absolute basics of shelter and hearth, in contrast to "cottage," or (in Downing's words) a "house of limited accommodation" but house nonetheless, with antecedents in city and town rather than tent and fire. Both cottage and camp ultimately arrive at the same place, an opening through which nature and built environment freely communicate, but they arrive from opposite sides of the threshold.

Brickelmeyer Cottage, Randolph, New Hampshire, (J. H. Boothman, 1914), kitchen entry with latticed vestibule.

It was not until I started to search in earnest among the older houses for those that might fit my initial ideas of camp or cottage that I realized how little, by contrast, modern summer houses resemble either type. I wondered about this at some length, particularly as I learned to distinguish exactly what made the attractive old houses "work." Whatever was lacking in most modern vacation houses was not obviously architectural. The answer eventually came to me, not in a house but in a commercial campground where I was tenting in the course of a photography trip. I was surrounded by enormous recreational vehicles, most of which were set up for a long stay, tires draped in special covers, lawn furniture under awnings, little yards marked by a decorative fence, a strip of AstroTurf covering the grass. Air conditioners hummed at the backs of vehicles, and in the evening dusk, blue light streamed from televisions inside the vehicles. Here it occurred to me that while my neighbors were on vacation, no less than the rusticators of Mt. Desert or the original occupants of the houses I was photographing, there was a difference: these campers had brought all the impediments and conveniences of their everyday lives with them. It was a vacation only in the limited sense of place and labor.

This is to me what distinguishes so many modern vacation houses from their antecedents: they have become merely appendages of the rest of life. Once we are equipped with the conveniences and tools of modern life, with Internet, television, washing machines, air conditioners, and cell phones, regardless of where we are located, to what degree are we on vacation? Surrounded by so much of the paraphernalia of our daily life, how far are we removed from what we have vacated ourselves from, not physically but aesthetically and spiritually, from whatever obligations and irritations we seek refuge from? Can we expect to find, as the rusticators found, renewal in a clearer appreciation of the world?

I am mindful as I write this that we are fortunate if we have the opportunity to leave town at all, but it is worth considering what, given the chance, we take with us that might be better left behind. I write this as I sit in my old house, surrounded by forest and mountains but also by my computer, and through it all the resources, obligations, and distractions that the outside world offers. The architecture we surround

House by J. H. Boothman, Randolph, New Hampshire, with later alterations to enclose undercut porch.

ourselves with provides a setting for life, but what we *do* there depends on what life we choose to live in that setting. Shall we bring all the comforts and tools with us and simply continue working in a novel setting? Or shall we live a simpler life for a brief spell, like the Coolidge sons who rejected even mosquito netting between themselves and the nature they embraced, or the visitors to a cottage on a Maine island who gather around a single kerosene lamp in the evening? I believe we have the opportunity, even today, and in part through architecture, to follow the example of the small-town builders, to simplify and distill our lives, to identify and preserve essential elements, and discard others. Like the houses, which became simpler without loosing their aesthetic value, we can diminish our burdens without impoverishing our souls.

Bartlett Cottage, Randolph, New Hampshire (J. H. Boothman, 1919), porch in winter.

In those days the winter population of Randolph Hill was about six, counting me. I spent the short days walking or snowshoeing around the Hill, exploring the snow-filled woods and walking the roads, each summer cottage — save the few we winter residents occupied — shuttered, banked, and buried in snow. As I wandered, I became fascinated by the winter sky, by the snow, and as it turned out, by the town itself: by the houses spaced at wide intervals along the road, set back in forest or standing in a remnant of the pasture that, seventy years before, lay across the top of the entire Hill, everything open to sky and mountains.

My days were not clearly distinguished from each other. Weather more than anything

Brickelmeyer Cottage, Randolph, New Hampshire, (J. H. Boothman, 1914), outbuilding.

determined my activities. In an afternoon's outing I could go in any direction on the maze of Randolph's trails. The big peaks of Madison and Adams were visible from every part of the Hill, and almost every house was oriented to the south, facing that view. To the north of the Hill, forest continued across a shallow valley and up among the ledges of Mt. Crescent, covered by maple, poplar and birch, with lines of spruce and fir along the small streams running down the slope. High on Mt. Crescent the evergreens took over altogether, making a dense, dog-hair grove of tiny spruce and moss, shrouded in fog on the rainy days.

The top of the Hill road led most directly toward Mt. Crescent, and was a starting point for an excursion late one overcast January afternoon. Heading in this direction I passed a dozen closed-up houses; some new, some old, each tucked into its respective spot in the forest. At a point where the Hill road narrowed and turned to dirt I passed an old cabin sunk in its foundation and smelling of pine pitch in the cold air. Across the road on the north side, a larger, airy house from the 1920s – one of Boothman's houses – was set back in a meadow, pieces of the mountains reflected in its windows. Cedar shake siding, stained brown and black by water and time, stood out against the snow and late afternoon gray sky. Further along, a stand of white birches surrounded a tiny square cottage, clad also in cedar shakes, one end of the house undercut by a screen porch. A stone wall ran along the road in front, tumbled down, vanishing in places under the snow or scattered by the roots of a large maple. Farther along, I passed a wonderfully grace-

ful house with a fieldstone chimney, hipped roof and tight line of high, square, small-paned windows. Walking up and down this road in summer so many hundreds of times, I had paid no more attention to the houses than the forest, but now, alone in the silence of January, the houses became my closest company, carrying memories of people and history – my own as well as the histories of others.

Turning into the forest I followed a trail north through firs which opened up shortly into mature maples. The forest became taller as I entered a broad and shallow depression with a stream emerging from a spring at its center. This was Boothman Spring, about a quarter mile into the woods behind the Mt. Crescent House Hotel, out of business, but not yet torn down. Many years before, the hotel had held evening cookouts here, roasting corn on a fire beside the spring. These occasions ended a long time ago, and my memory of them was vague. I recognized a great flat-topped boulder beside the spring, and gauged the age of my memory by the diminished size of the rock. The light of recollection is often more vivid and more colorful than the original scene, and the far-off voices and faces coming to back to me at Boothman Spring glowed in comparison to the failing light in the woods.

Back out on the road I turned east and walked along the broad level top of the Hill. The air smelled of snow. The bare branches of maple and beech trees stood against the sky. Houses, fields, and road all appeared flat and slightly distant both in space and time, lit by the fading and anonymous light. The houses I passed all held some memory for me.

Randolph has changed along with the rest of the world, and the houses have changed and are changing with it. The winter population of the Hill is much greater today, and one consequence is that the houses whose shape and colors I treasure are vanishing under insulation and

Brickelmeyer Cottage, Randolph, New Hampshire, (J. H. Boothman, 1914), winter view.

drywall and all the modern renovations that any sensible person will make to a house in order to live in comfort through a New Hampshire winter.

And I too have been gone from New Hampshire nearly thirty years now; my winter there and my wanderings among the houses are now memories themselves. I have returned to look at these houses again, perhaps to understand what makes them what they are to me, but at least to study them and fix them in my memory, before they disappear, displaced by renovation and lost to memory — as a person on waking tells a dream before it slips out of consciousness, out of memory, simultaneously remembered and forgotten.

"The Mousetrap," Randolph, New Hampshire, builder unknown.

ACKNOWLEDGMENTS

One unexpected benefit of writing a book like *The Hand of the Small-Town Builder* turns out to be the number and variety of people one meets along the way. What started out as a modest photo essay evolved into a decade-long research project that led me to hundreds of people, from house owners and historians to carpenters, foresters, genealogists, architects, preservationists, and, especially, communities. Summer communities across northern New England are connected across time and space by shared values, common geographic and economic origins, and parallel experiences. I never found two communities that were interchangeable in any way, but I always found common elements: aspects of a community's origins, or of its members, that rhymed or resonated with another's, sometimes with startling closeness.

I cannot do justice here to the generosity and friendship offered to me during this project, but I can try to give an idea of its scope. First and foremost, I am indebted to the owners of the houses I photographed, but whom, for their privacy, I will not name. Their generosity in inviting a stranger to come into their homes was striking, and not least in the quickness with which they understood and shared my interests. This is understandable, for those people who kept their houses in the traditional forms that most interested me had done so for exactly the same reasons that I had for wanting to photograph them.

Local historians were not only extraordinarily valuable sources of information, but also typically served as my point of entry into a community. My approach in seeking houses was, most often, to contact a local historical society or historian in a region and describe my interests; my local contact could then tell me if their town or region had the types of houses I was interested in. They could also make initial inquiries of the owners on my behalf; in this way initial contacts with the owners could be made without my direct involvement, and owners could decline anonymously if they desired. (Most didn't.)

Barbara Rumsey, of the Boothbay (Maine) Historical Society, and Mary Jones of the Southwest Harbor (Maine) and a former member of the Maine Architectural Preservation Commission, were among my very first contacts, and became my most trusted historical advisers and strictest critics concerning the pitfalls of careless history (although those errors still lurking in this story are entirely my own responsibility). For regional historical guidance I am also indebted to Earle Shettleworth, of the Maine Historic Preservation Commission, James Garvin of the New Hampshire Division of Historical Resources, and Elsa Gilbertson of the Vermont Division for Historic Preservation. In the many towns I visited, historians and dedicated and knowledgeable residents volunteered their time, knowledge, experience, and often their hospitality as well. I am indebted in all these respects to Kitty Anagnost, Joan Barton, Polly Beatie, Clive Gray, Al and Judy Hudson, Nancy and Don Mairs, Martha Mayo, Tedd and Dorothy Osgood, Tom Pears, Liz Prichett, Gary Priest, Phil Reilly, Gail and Hugh Sangree, Jack Schultz, Lacie Smith, Wilhemina Smith, Bryant Tolles, Pat and John Waldman, and Cathie Wilkinson.

For discussions on architecture and expertise in matters of the houses themselves, ranging from 19th century architectural history to the detailed workings of a carpenter's crew 100 years ago, I am indebted to John, David, and Robert Anderson, Susanna Blachley, Eric Henry, Ken Hutchins, John Mackin, Vince Mancuso,

Randolph, New Hampshire, beech trees in winter.

and Morris Norwood. For good advice, inspiration, and many stimulating conversations on photography I am also indebted to George DeWolfe, James Balog, Robert Anderson, Chris Brown, and William Napier.

For information on Robie Norwood, and Sylvanus Morgan I benefited enormously from documents and personal histories from Norwood's granddaughter Susan Hodge and Morgan's granddaughter Anne Riggs, both of whom generously provided their time and memories.

For information on John Boothman and access to the Boothman family's extensive records, I am similarly indebted to John Boothman's granddaughters Susan Hawkins, Sarah Glines, and Rebecca Boothman. I thank these three also for years of shared memory and experience.

The evolution of this book from a casual photography project depended critically on one organization and three people. Some ten years ago, when I was photographing some of John Boothman's houses for my own pleasure, Boothman's granddaughter Susan Hawkins was considering writing a biography of him, and some discussions of our common interests led to our considering a joint project. Sue's enthusiasm and vision provided the lift that raised our ideas from a hobby to a goal; Sue's hand (like the builder's) is present in the final work. Later, while searching for a publisher, provided with only a very slim folder of photographs, I received valuable advice and encouragement from my friend Carl Zahn, as well as an introduction to David Godine. It was David who urged me to broaden my vision beyond a single builder and a single town, setting me on the path that, winding through history and architecture, ultimately led to this book in its present form.

Another lift at a critical moment came through a grant from the Graham Foundation for Advanced Studies in the Fine Arts, which supported the first several years of this work.

Finally, my family has had a role in this effort, even beyond the forbearance that all preoccupied authors ask of their loved ones. They have worked with me scouting locations, carrying equipment, assisting in the photography, meeting owners, and generally carrying the whole project forward. My parents had a role as well, choosing to stay in Randolph, New Hampshire (a spur of the moment decision: they were originally headed for Vermont) some sixty years ago. Finally, my greatest thanks go to my wife Anne, my first source of editorial and critical advice and companion in a journey that led through many houses and many lives.

NOTES

NEW ENGLANDERS IN SUMMER

1 Northern New England was almost entirely wilderness (from the European's point of view) until after the French and Indian War in the 1760s. Settlement extended rapidly into the interior of New England in the last decades of the eighteenth century, but travel during these years was not generally regarded as anything to be taken up as a matter of pleasure.

2 Many histories recount the exploration and early settlement of the White Mountains. *Lucy Crawford's History of the White Mountains* (Dartmouth Publications: Hanover, New Hampshire, 1966) is a famous near-contemporary account of this period.

3 East of the Kennebec River, the crenulated Maine coastline, cut by rivers, bays, and inlets, and with settlements often placed at sheltered harbors at the outer ends of the peninsulas, was intrinsically inhospitable to the construction of railroad lines. Wagon roads were forced to take circuitous routes to link places closely connected by water. Even as late as 1917, in an exceptionally cold winter, the townspeople of Boothbay, struck down by a flu epidemic, were trapped when their sole source of winter transportation – boats – were immobilized as the harbor froze.

4 *Among the White Hills: The Life and Time of Guy L. Shorey.* Guy A. Gosselin and Susan B. Hawkins. Peter E. Randall: Portsmouth, New Hampshire, 1998.

5 *Chronicles of the White Mountains.* Fredrick F. Kilbourne. Houghton Mifflin, Co.: Boston, 1916.

6 *Guide to Moosehead Lake and Northern Maine.* Anonymous. Bradford and Anthony: Boston, 1874.

7 *Chronicles of the White Mountains.* Fredrick F. Kilbourne. Houghton Mifflin, Co.: Boston, 1916.

8 *The History of Greensboro: The First 200 Years.* Greensboro Historical Society, 1990.

9 *Working at Play: A History of Vacations in the United States.* Cindy S. Aron. Oxford University Press, 1999, p. 33. Aron gives a comprehensive picture of the fascinating social and economic evolution of vacations in the United States.

10 *Ibid.* Ironically, but perhaps not surprisingly, vacations were initially thought of as being of value only to workers whose chief responsibilities were intellectual; the benefit of rest for those whose labors were merely physical was somehow overlooked.

ORIGINS OF THE SUMMER HOUSE

1 The nineteenth-century development of a uniquely American domestic architecture has been extensively documented and analyzed. Vincent Scully's *The Shingle Style and the Stick Style: Architectural Theory and Design from Downing to the Origins of Wright* (Yale University Press, rev. ed., 1971) is the definitive study of this period, and like all writers on architecture from this period, I draw heavily on Scully. My focus is limited, however, and I concentrate on those parts of this history most relevant to the emergence of a vernacular summer architecture with origins in Queen Anne, Stick, and Shingle styles between 1870 and 1935.

2 Massing and articulation are basic building blocks of architectural design and were among the properties of building most altered by nineteenth-century architectural developments. "Massing" refers to the expression of interior volumes in the external forms of a building, while "articulation" refers to the ways in which massed components of a building are joined together.

3 *A Treatise on the Theory and Practice of Landscape Gardening, Adapted to North America.* Andrew Jackson Downing. C. C. Little & Co.: Boston, 1841; *Cottage Residences: or, A Series of Designs for Rural Cottages and Cottage Villas, and Their Gardens and Grounds, Adapted to North America.* Wiley & Halsted: New York, 1842; *The Architecture of Country Houses; Including Designs for Cottages, Farm-Houses, and Villas, with Remarks on Interiors, Furniture, and the Best Modes of Warming and Ventilating.* D. Appleton & Co.: New York, 1850.

4 Until 1854, when American Commodore Matthew Perry forced the opening of diplomatic and commercial exchange, Japan had been closed to the West for more than two centuries. The inclusion of two Japanese buildings in the Philadelphia Centennial Exhibition of 1876 created an immediate, intense, and widespread interest in Japanese architecture. This interest was reinforced by the English translation in the same year of Eugène Viollet-le-Duc's influential book *The Habitations of Man in All Ages* (B. Bucknall, trans. J. R. Osgood and Company, 1876).

5 Photo: Library of Congress, Prints & Photographs Division, HABS. Cervin Robinson, Photographer, September 18, 1962, HABS RI,1-BRIST,18-3.

6 The history of builder's guides, plan books, mail-order plans, precut houses, and all the other instruments by which nineteenth- and twentieth-century architecture was communicated to an expanding American population is a fascinating and complex story in itself. I do not attempt to describe the

full variety and magnitude of this enterprise here, but Daniel D. Reiff's *Houses from Books* (The Pennsylvania State University Press: Philadelphia, 2001) tells this story in detail, as well as documenting many extant examples of houses built from particular plans. Reiff also delves into the actual practices of local builders, revealing how their own skills and sensibilities added to the diversity and maturation of American domestic architecture at this time. Two other valuable investigations into this history are Kathryn Dethier's "The Spirit of Progressive Reform: *The Ladies' Home Journal* House Plans, 1900–1902" (*Journal of Design History* 6(4), 1993) and James L. Garvin's "Mail-Order House Plans and American Victorian Architecture" (*Winterthur Portfolio* 16(4), 1981).

7   Alexander Jackson Davis published *Rural Residences* in 1837, and Andrew Jackson Downing published *Cottage Residences* in 1842, the first of seven editions.

8   Well-known examples of these publications include M.F. Cummings and C.C. Miller's *Architecture: Designs for Street Fronts, Suburban Houses, and Cottages, Including Details for Both Exterior and Interior* (A.J. Bicknell: Troy, New York, 1868).

MAINE COAST

1   *Colonial Boothbay: Mid-1600s to 1775.* B. Rumsey. Winnegance House: East Boothbay, Maine, 2000.

2   It is not possible in a few paragraphs to do justice to the important issue of the historical influence of tourism on Maine's (indeed all of northern New England's) economy. Colin Woodard's excellent book *The Lobster Coast* (Pengiun Books: New York, 2004) provides an extensive discussion of the human dimension of the economic influence of coastal Maine tourism, a dimension that architecture alone does not tell us much about.

3   *History of Boothbay, Southport, and Boothbay Harbor.* Francis B. Greene. Loring, Short, and Harmon: Portland, Maine, 1906.

4   *An Historical Survey of Ocean Point Architecture.* C. K. Anagnost and H. A. Pinkham. Privately published: Ocean Point, Maine, 1991.

5   *Ibid.*

6   Scully, for example, describes Bruce Price's "The Craigs" (1879–1880) at Mt. Desert Island as "without discipline . . . hearty, violent, and free." *The Shingle Style and the Stick Style: Architectural Theory and Design from Downing to the Origins of Wright.* V. Scully. Yale University Press, rev. ed., 1971.

7   "Squirrel Island Semi-Centennial." Ethan Allen Chase. *Lewiston Journal Magazine*, 1921.

8   *Ibid.*

9   See *Maine Cottages: Fred L. Savage and the Architecture of Mt. Desert.* John M. Bryan. Princeton Architectural Press, 2005.

10   *Cyclopedia of American Biography.* James T. White, 1899. Fernald was a well-known natural scientist in his day, and his life and career can be traced in a variety of sources, including archive files at the University of Massachusetts at Amherst.

11   Industrialization and compartmentalization of labor in the nineteenth century broke down traditional master–apprentice relationships, and by the late 1800s apprenticeships in the formal sense no longer existed in New England trades. Nevertheless, any young craftsman would learn by working with an established master craftsman for some years before establishing an independent operation.

12   Letter from Hope Norwood Bannister, ca. 1987, collection of Susan Hodge.

13   My sources of information on Norwood's carpentry business are anecdotal but come from several sources who were employed by Norwood, knew him personally, or who have worked on his houses. I am particularly indebted to Morris Norwood, Ken Hutchins, and Eric Henry, all of Southwest Harbor, and to Norwood's granddaughter, Mrs. Susan Hodge.

14   *History of Yard Lumber Size Standards.* L. W. Smith and L. W. Wood. Forest Products Laboratory, Forest Service, U.S. Dept. of Agriculture, 1964.

15   Evidence for this imprecision can be seen in many buildings of this time, where exposed studs and joists are laid out on only roughly regular intervals.

16   Morris Norwood interview, 26 July 2006, Southwest Harbor, Maine.

17   Much of my information on specific house details is drawn from Deborah Thompson's *Historic Resource Inventories of the Town of Southwest Harbor and Somesville, Mt. Desert Island, Maine, Parts One and Two.* 1998–99 and 1999–2000. Unpublished. (Available at Town Office, Southwest Harbor, Maine, Southwest Harbor Public Library, and Mt. Desert Historical Society).

18   Deborah Thompson, *op cit.*

19   Daniel D. Reiff, *Houses from Books.* The Pennsylvania State University Press: Philadelphia, 2001.

20   "American Vernacular Architecture, IV," *The American Architect and Building News*, 6 July 1878.

21   Collection of Rachel Cope Evans family.

INLAND MAINE

1   Maine was a part of Massachusetts until 1820. The geography of the area and its resources were roughly known from the travels of Lt. John Montresor in the 1760s and Benedict Arnold's expedition to Quebec City in 1775–76.

2   "Students Island," on Mooselookmeguntic Lake, is named for a group of Yale undergraduates who came to fish at Rangeley during this early period.

3   *Brook Trout Fishing: An Account of a Trip of the Oquossuc Angling Association to Northern Maine.* R. G. Allerton. Paris and Brown: New York, 1869. Rangeley's brook trout attained their enormous size because of the abundance of another species, blueback trout, on which the brook trout fed. The bluebacks were wiped out in the early twentieth century, and the big brook trout with them, as a consequence of the earlier introduction of landlocked salmon.

4   This anecdote may be a conflation of events – a fish story, in fact – but from Allerton's account it is clear that Agassiz was consulted on the fish at Rangeley. Agassiz's personal library at Harvard also contained a copy of Allerton's book, inscribed to Agassiz by the author.

5   Guidebooks to the Rangeley region were abundant, regularly revised, and appeared as books, pamphlets, and magazine articles. Many of the guidebooks were diverse, heterogeneous (and heavy) compilations of factual geographic data, railroad timetables, maps, discussions of fishing methods and paraphernalia, effusive accounts of camp life, and general exhortations on the merits of fishing as sport. One good example is "Farrar's Illustrated Guide Book to the Androscoggin Lakes," published by Lee and Shepard, Boston, in 1890.

6   For a good account of Crosby's life and early Maine tourism, see *Fly Rod Crosby: the woman who marketed Maine* (Julia A. Hunter and Earle G. Shettleworth Jr., Tillbury House Publishers, 2000).

7   *Ibid.*

8   "We do not look for wallpaper or carpets in our tiny rooms upstairs, and we are not disappointed. Thin board partitions permit the slightest sound to be heard throughout the house – a circumstance calculated to promote sociable intercourse." From Ripley Hitchcock, "Fishing in Maine," *Outing Magazine*, vol. 7, May 1886.

9   This same style of spatial organization appears in mountain huts in Europe and the U.S., including the Appalachian Mountain Club's huts in New Hampshire's White Mountains. The communal use and shared interests of the clientele of the mountain huts is parallel to those in the fishing camps.

10 Harvey Kaiser's *Great Camps of the Adirondacks* (David R. Godine, 1982) tells the story of the development of nineteenth-century tourism in this region, as well as the rise – and decline – of these distinctive and monumental buildings.

11 "'An ideal life in the woods for boys'. Architecture and Culture in the Earliest Summer Camps," W. Barksdale Maynard, *Winterthur Portfolio* 34(1), 1999. This connection is explored further in Chapter 5 on Squam Lake.

12 This is my own definition of the distinction between "camp" and "cottage," based as nearly as I can on origins; one term or the other tends to be strongly preferred in any given locality, and the choice doesn't necessarily conform to my – or any – rule. In fact, the terms are slowly losing their meaning as modern summer houses become indistinguishable from year-round houses. The terms are muddled even more by the occasional appearance of the label "camp cottage."

13 "Gilded Summers in Belgrade, Maine," John Mundt, *The American Fly Fisher* 26(3), 2000. Keliher's Winona Beach camp started as a single cabin but was built specifically as a commercial venture. The camp was later sold to Albert Clifford, who operated the business under the name Messalonskee Beach Camps.

14 *Ibid.* Letter dated April 20, 1831, in *The American Turf Register and Sporting Magazine.* The author of the letter ("J.R.P.," from Augusta) refers only to trout fishing.

15 "The coming summer will witness many additions to the list of private cottage owners as well as extensions of the various sporting camps which are growing in popularity." From article entitled, "Cottage Extensions at Belgrade," *Northward Ho!* 8(10), p. 27, 1912.

16 The Adirondack style was still being defined and gaining fame in 1901, but many of the early and classic camps, such as those at Raquette Lake, had been built twenty or more years before and would have been known to an architect with an interest in rustic design. See *Great Camps of the Adirondacks* (Harvey Kaiser, David R. Godine, 1982).

17 Trapper's camps in Alaska and Canada during and before this era were normally built with some number of isolated structures explicitly for fire protection. Fire was an especially threatening hazard in remote northern places, for the loss of one's shelter in winter would be just as deadly as the fire itself. Trappers, hunters, and prospectors routinely kept a small second cabin (or at least a cache) stocked with clothing, food, and tools at permanent winter camps.

NEW HAMPSHIRE

1   Darby Field's extraordinary expedition to the summit of Mount Washington in 1642 is the great anomaly in this pattern. In eighteen days, Field, accompanied by several Indian companions, made his way east along the coast forty miles to the mouth of the Saco River, and thence upstream another sixty miles to Conway and ultimately to the summit of Mount Washington, the first recorded mountaineering ascent in North American history 144 years before the first ascent of Mont Blanc.

2   The excavation of the Neville Site, on the Merrimack River near Manchester, yielded archeological evidence of occupation going back 8,000 years. *The Neville Site: 8,000 Years at Amoskeag, Manchester, New Hampshire.* Dena Ferran Dincauze. Harvard University Press, 2005.

3   "'An Ideal Life in the Woods for Boys': Architecture and Culture in the Earliest Summer Camps." W. Barksdale Maynard. *Winterthur Portfolio* 34(1), 1999.

4   Thomas Cole's first trip to the White Mountains was in 1827, for example, only sixty-four years after the end of the French and Indian War.

5   "American Landscape: Changing Concepts of the Sublime." B. Novak. *American Art Journal* 4(1), 1972.

6   I am indebted to the present owner of Winter Road Hill for research on the history of the Cummings and Howe families' residence at Silver Lake, on the details of the building and ownership of the house itself, and on the vibrant intellectual community that met under its roof. Among the many writers, artists, and intellectuals who were guests at Winter Road Hill was the photographer Eliot Porter, who stayed at the house while photographing at Silver Lake for his landmark book *In Wildness is the Preservation of the World.*

7   The White Mountains hotel culture in general, and Randolph history in particular, are chronicled in a number of sources. *Forest and Crag: A History of Hiking, Trail Blazing, and Adventure in the Northeast Mountains* (Laura and Guy Waterman, Appalachian Mountain Club Books, Boston, 1989) gives an encyclopedic account of the hiking and trail building traditions of the northeast. George N. Cross's *Randolph Old and New* (privately published, 1929) provides an anecdotal history of Randolph from its earliest days to the first decades of the twentieth century. A more historically authoritative history of the northern White Mountains – up through 1888 only – is available in reissue in the *History of Coös County* (New Hampshire Publishing Co., 1972).

8   Letter, J.H. Boothman to H. L. Malcolm, January 3, 1939. "Mr. Pote" was Winston Pote, of Sugar Hill, a son-in-law of Boothman's and well-known mountain and ski photographer of the day. Boothman family papers.

9   Obituary, *Berlin Reporter*, November 26, 1952.

10 *Ibid.*

11 Berlin City Directories, 1903, 1909, 1915, 1920, 1924. Moffett House Museum: Berlin, New Hampshire.

12 There is a consistent pattern of house types that can be seen nearly everywhere in northern New England: earlier development (late eighteenth to early nineteenth century) occurred first along the rivers and along the perimeter of broad arable flood plains, and in these locations Post-Colonial and Greek Revival tend to dominate. Later, mid-nineteenth century development was focused on the sources of water power – the waterfalls on the rivers, and at these locations Queen Anne, Italianate, and French Second Empire become more noticeable, and finally, in locations with late-century industrial development, eclectic combinations proliferate, using forms borrowed from the full breadth of Victorian styles as well as Colonial Revival, most often in new construction, but also as renovations and re-workings of existing buildings.

13 In 1900, Berlin had a population of nearly 9,000 people, increased from 6,000 only four years before. By 1913 the population had risen to 14,000. The city's forest industry began a shift from lumber to pulp processing and paper making in 1897, and Berlin remained a world leader in the development of pulp and paper technology until the 1960s.

14 The Mt. Crescent House opened its doors in 1888, well before the earliest known private cottages were built. John Boothman bought the Mt. Crescent House in 1918, and it remained in the Boothman family until its final closure in 1971.

15 M. H. Baillie-Scott. George Newnes, London, 1906, reprinted 2004 by Antique Collector's Club, LTD.

16 Interview of Freeman Holden by Susan Hawkins, August 14, 2000.

17 The total costs at the time of this writing, in 2007 dollars, would be $89,500 (calculated by deflated GDP). Boothman's day rate in 2007 dollars (and relative to other salaries in his day) would have been $174.

18 Information on Boothman's houses, complete as it is, contains some frustrating (and tantalizing) holes. While he is believed to have built about eighty-five houses in Randolph, many are only informally ascribed to him. The documentation of his houses is patchy, and the dates of construction where documents don't exist are mostly guesses aided by anecdotes and memory. Boothman probably built many houses in Randolph during the nine-year period between 1905 and 1914, but clear documentation and drawings exist for only one (built in 1912). I have not attempted to make a complete inventory of Boothman's buildings and have used only selected examples of his confirmed work in this discussion.

19 See, for example, *Craftsman Homes* by Gustav Stickley (self-published, 1909).

20 The determination of framing appropriate for anticipated structural loads, a ubiquitous part of architectural plans today (and required, for the record, to satisfy most local building codes), was not carried out by architects a century ago. Builders were assumed to have the requisite knowledge for designing structures appropriately, but in addition to this, building materials were much more variable. Not only did lumber sizing vary regionally in the late nineteenth and the first decades of the twentieth century, but lumber species vary in their intrinsic strength, so that framing details would depend upon the sawn size and types of wood available in any particular location.

21 *Ladies' Home Journal*, in 7 parts, 1902–1905.

22 See "The Spirit of Progressive Reform: *The Ladies' Home Journal* House Plans, 1900–1902," K. Dethier. *Journal of Design History* 6(4), 1993.

23 "[H]e and his sons did most of the work on the house." Bradley's daughter Fern Bradley Dufner, 1978, describing construction of Bradley house in Millburn, New Jersey, ca. 1915

(*Millburn-Short Hills New Jersey Historical Society* 5(3), May 1981).

24 Eldena Hunt diary, July 9, 1906. In *The Randolph Diaries of Eldena Leighton Hunt*, transcribed and edited by Joan Hunt Hall and Al Hudson, Randolph, New Hampshire: Randolph History Project, 2007 (v. 1), 2008 (v. 2).

25 In another Randolph case where Boothman used an architect's plan (W. H. P. Hatch cottage, W. Nelson Wilkins, architect, Boston, 1920), standard sixteen-inch stud and joist patterns were indicated, but Boothman changed the framing to his more typical open style with larger members.

26 Freeman Holden (1912–2001), who worked on Boothman's crew from 1944 to Boothman's death in 1953, recalled the ordering and delivery of lumber: "A lot of the lumber came from Gorham to Randolph Station by train. [Boothman] would order lumber for an entire house, they'd saw it out, when they got it sawn out they load it up on a flat car and send it up, and they'd haul it up to the house." Interview with Susan Boothman Hawkins, August 14, 2000.

27 E.g. Wells-MacFarlane house (Randolph, J. H. Boothman, 1912).

28 Merrill, Georgia D., *History of Coös County*. W. A. Fergusson and Co.: Boston, 1888, p. 85. Reprinted 1972 by New Hampshire Publishing Company: Somersworth, New Hampshire.

29 "A Lost Town: A Sketch of Bethlehem." George H. Moses. *The Granite Monthly* 17(1), July 1894.

30 *Ibid*.

31 The history and career of S. D. Morgan has been discussed extensively in Bryant Tolles' books, *The Grand Resort Hotels of the White Mountains* (David R. Godine, 1998), and *Summer Cottages of the White Mountains* (University Press of New England, 2000).

32 A number of New England hoteliers followed the practice of running establishments seasonally in the north and south. Herbert Malcolm, Randolph summer resident and friend of John Boothman, owned the Waumbek Hotel in Jefferson, New Hampshire, and the Hillsboro Club near Pompano Beach, Florida.

33 The California architects Greene and Greene, after Gustav Stickley perhaps the most well-known and influential practitioners of the Craftsman style, were at the height of their popularity in the years 1902–1910.

VERMONT

1 James Whitelaw, 1796. Survey of the Bayley–Hazen road.

2 Greensboro's history, from its earliest days to the early 1990s, is told in *The History of Greensboro – The First Two Hundred Years* (Greensboro Historical Society, 1990). The list of artisans and merchants in Greensboro at the start of the nineteenth century testifies to the town's self-sufficiency, characteristic of New England towns in an age when skills and materials had to be locally available to be of use. By ca. 1810, Greensboro had, among other enterprises, three sawmills, two gristmills, an oat mill, and a shingle mill. By the late 1800s, skilled labor in town included a tinsmith, cooper, basket maker, buttertub maker, leather and harness maker, blacksmith, and a variety of carpenters, carriage makers, and other metal and wood workers.

3 I am drawing here on conversations with Greensboro residents Lacie Smith, Joan Barton, and John Mackin, who generously shared their knowledge of George Fowler's personality as well as his building methods.

4 *The History of Greensboro – The First Two Hundred Years* (Greensboro Historical Society, 1990).

5 The expression of the Progressive movement and the Reform Era in architecture is explored by Gwendolyn Wright in *Moralism and the Model Home* (University of Chicago Press, 1980). Broader views of the Reform Era are presented in *Ministers of Reform: The Progressives' Achievement in American Civilization, 1889–1920* (Robert M. Crunden, Basic Books, New York, 1982) and in Richard Hofstadter's classic, *The Age of Reform* (Random House, 1955).

6 Jesse Bancroft was a noted authority in children's physical education, serving as director of physical education for the Brooklyn, New York, public schools (1893–1903) and later as assistant director of physical training for the New York City public school system (1904–1928).

EPILOGUE

1 Rizzoli International, New York, 1989.

SELECTED BIBLIOGRAPHY

Aaron, Cindy S. *Working at Play: A History of Vacations in the United States.* Oxford University Press: New York, 1999.

Allerton, R. G. *Brook Trout Fishing. An Account of a Trip of the Oquossuc Angling Association to Northern Maine.* Paris and Brown: New York, 1869.

Anagnost, C. K. and H. A. Pinkham. *An Historical Survey of Ocean Point Architecture.* Privately published: Ocean Point, Maine, 1991.

Anonymous. "American Vernacular Architecture, IV." *The American Architect and Building News.* 6 July 1878.

Anonymous. "Cottage Extensions at Belgrade." *Northward Ho!* 8 (10), p. 27, 1912.

Anonymous. *Guide to Moosehead Lake and Northern Maine.* Bradford and Anthony: Boston, 1874.

Bradley, Will. "A Bradley House." *Ladies' Home Journal*, in 7 parts, 1902-1905.

Bryan, John M. *Maine Cottages: Fred L. Savage and the Architecture of Mt. Desert.* Princeton Architectural Press: Princeton, NJ, 2005.

Chase, Ethan Allen. *Lewiston Journal Magazine*, 1921.

Crawford, Lucy. *Lucy Crawford's History of the White Mountains.* Dartmouth Publications: Hanover, New Hampshire, 1966.

Cross, George N. *Randolph Old and New.* Privately published, 1929.

Crunden, Robert M. *Ministers of Reform: The Progressives' Achievement in American Civilization, 1889–1920.* Basic Books: New York, 1982.

Cummings, M.F., and C. C. Miller. *Architecture: Designs for Street Fronts, Suburban Houses, and Cottages, Including Details for Both Exterior and Interior.* A. J. Bicknell: Troy, New York, 1868.

Davis, Alexander Jackson. *Rural Residences: Consisting of Designs, Original and Selected, for Cottages, Farm-houses, Villas, and Village Churches, with Brief Explanations, Estimates, and a Specification of Materials, Construction, Etc.* New York University, 1837 (reissued, Da Capo Press, 1980).

Dethier, Kathryn. "The Spirit of Progressive Reform: *The Ladies' Home Journal* House Plans, 1900–1902." *Journal of Design History* 6 (4), 1993.

Dincauze, Dena Ferran. *The Neville Site: 8,000 Years at Amoskeag, Manchester, New Hampshire.* Harvard University Press: Cambridge, MA, 2005.

Downing, Andrew Jackson. *The Architecture of Country Houses; Including Designs for Cottages, Farm-Houses, and Villas, with Remarks on Interiors, Furniture, and the Best Modes of Warming and Ventilating.* D. Appleton & Co.: New York, 1850 (reissued, Dover, 1969).

Downing, Andrew Jackson. *Cottage Residences: or, A Series of Designs for Rural Cottages and Cottage Villas, and Their Gardens and Grounds, Adapted to North America.* Wiley & Halsted: New York, 1842 and subsequent editions (reissued, Dover, 1981).

Downing, Andrew Jackson. *A Treatise on the Theory and Practice of Landscape Gardening, Adapted to North America.* C.C. Little & Co.: Boston, 1841 (reissued, Nabu Press, 2010).

Farrar, Charles A. J., *Farrar's Illustrated Guide Book to the Androscoggin Lakes.* Lee and Shepard: Boston, 1890.

Garvin, James L. "Mail-Order House Plans and American Victorian Architecture." *Winterthur Portfolio* 16(4), 1981.

Gosselin, Guy A., and Susan B. Hawkins. *Among the White Hills: The Life and Time of Guy L. Shorey.* Peter E. Randall: Portsmouth, New Hampshire, 1998.

Greene, Francis B. *History of Boothbay, Southport, and Boothbay Harbor.* Loring, Short, and Harmon: Portland, Maine, 1906.

Greensboro Historical Society. *The History of Greensboro: The First 200 Years.* 1990.

Hall, Joan Hunt and Al Hudson, eds. *The Randolph Diaries of Eldena Leighton Hunt.* Randolph, New Hampshire: Randolph History Project, 2007 (1), 2008 (2).

Hitchcock, Ripley. "Fishing in Maine." *Outing Magazine*, vol. 7, May 1886.

Hofstadter, Richard. *The Age of Reform.* Random House, 1955.

Hunter, Julia A., and Earle G. Shettleworth Jr. *Fly Rod Crosby: the woman who marketed Maine.* Tillbury House Publishers, 2000.

Kaiser, Harvey. *Great Camps of the Adirondacks.* David R. Godine: Boston, 1982.

Kilbourne, Fredrick F. *Chronicles of the White Mountains.* Houghton Mifflin, Co.: Boston, 1916.

Maynard, W. Barksdale. "'An ideal life in the woods for boys': Architecture and Culture in the Earliest Summer Camps." *Winterthur Portfolio* 34(1), 1999.

Merrill, Georgia D. *History of Coös County.* W. A. Fergusson and Co.: Boston, 1888, p. 85. Reprinted 1972 by New Hampshire Publishing Company: Somersworth, New Hampshire.

Moses, George H. "A Lost Town: A Sketch of Bethlehem." *The Granite Monthly* 17(1), July 1894.

Mundt, John. "Gilded Summers in Belgrade, Maine." *The American Fly Fisher* 26(3), 2000.

Novak, B. "American Landscape. Changing Concepts of the Sublime." *American Art Journal* 4(1), 1972.

Reiff, Daniel D. *Houses from Books.* Penn State University Press: Philadelphia, 2001.

Rumsey, Barbara. *Colonial Boothbay: Mid-1600s to 1775.* Winnegance House: East Boothbay, Maine, 2000.

Scully, Vincent. *The Architecture of the American Summer: The Flowering of the Shingle Style.* Rizzoli International, 1989.

Scully, Vincent. *The Shingle Style and the Stick Style: Architectural Theory and Design from Downing to the Origins of Wright*, Yale University Press, rev. ed., 1971.

Smith, L. W. and L. W. Wood. *History of Yard Lumber Size Standards.* Forest Products Laboratory, Forest Service, U.S. Dept. of Agriculture, 1964.

Stickley, Gustav. *Craftsman Homes.* Self-published, 1909.

The History of Greensboro – The First Two Hundred Years. Greensboro Historical Society, 1990.

Thompson, Deborah. *Historic Resource Inventories of the Town of Southwest Harbor and Somesville, Mt. Desert Island, Maine, Parts One and Two.* 1998–99 and 1999–2000. Unpublished. (Available at Town Office, Southwest Harbor, Maine, Southwest Harbor Public Library, and Mt. Desert Historical Society.)

Tolles, Bryant. *Summer Cottages of the White Mountains.* University Press of New England, 2000.

Tolles, Bryant. *The Grand Resort Hotels of the White Mountains.* David R. Godine: Boston, 1998.

Viollet-le-Duc, Eugène. *The Habitations of Man in All Ages*, trans. B. Bucknall. J. R. Osgood and Company, 1876.

Waterman, Laura and Guy Waterman. *Forest and Crag: A History of Hiking, Trail Blazing, and Adventure in the Northeast Mountains.* Appalachian Mountain Club Books: Boston, 1989.

White, James T. *Cyclopedia of American Biography.* 1899.

Woodard, Colin. *The Lobster Coast.* Penguin Books: New York, 2004.

Wright, Gwendolyn. *Moralism and the Model Home.* University of Chicago Press: Chicago, 1980.

A NOTE ON THE TYPE

THE HAND OF THE SMALL-TOWN BUILDER *has been set in Monotype Columbus, a family of types designed by Patricia Saunders to commemorate the five-hundredth anniversary of their namesake's epic journey in search of a westward route to the Indies. The letterforms of these stylish types derive from two great Spanish printed books of the late fifteenth and early sixteenth centuries: one a collection of the works of Virgil printed by Jorge Coci, the other a calligraphic manual by Juan de Yciar, which featured types by the renowned French punchcutter Robert Granjon and was printed by Coci's son-in-law. In their current form, the Columbus types retain the lively, rather rustic flavor of their models, although the designer has judiciously modified elements that might interfere with comfortable reading. The types' rich color and sturdy forms are adaptable to a variety of books, but seem most at home when a decidedly decorative feel and dense texture are desired. ❧ The display capitals were designed by the German typographer E. R. Weiss.*

DESIGN & COMPOSITION BY
CARL W. SCARBROUGH

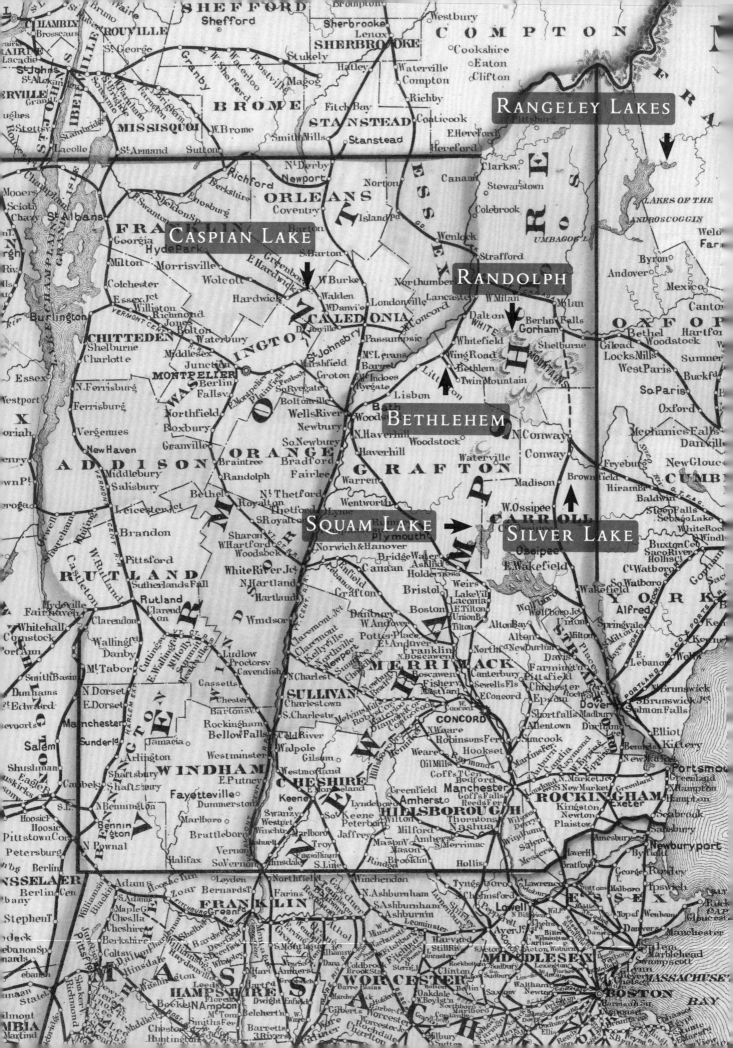